Table of Contents

	Page
Introduction by Tom Bethell	v
Chapter 1: Words & Phrases	1
1.1 Introduction	1
1.2 Words & Phrases--Entries	4
Chapter 2: Organizations	53
2.1 Introduction	53
2.2 Organizations--Entries	54
Appendix A: Government Actions and Press Freedom 1981-82	75
Appendix B: Selected Bibliography and Suggested Readings	83
Appendix C: U.S. Government--International Communications Policy	87
Index	93

International Communications Glossary

Timothy G. Brown
With an Introduction by Tom Bethell

the media institute
Washington, D.C.

International Communications Glossary

Copyright © 1984 The Media Institute

All rights reserved. No part of this publication may be reproduced or transmitted in any form without permission in writing from the publisher.

First printing November 1984.

Published by The Media Institute, Washington, D.C.

Printed in the United States of America.

ISBN: 0-937790-27-3

Library of Congress Catalog Card Number: 84-62298

Introduction

At one time the National Broadcasting Company put on an educational series called the "University of the Air," and included in the radio curriculum a weekly discussion of foreign policy. On June 1, 1946, as it happened, the topic was: "Is UNESCO the Key to International Understanding?" It turned out to be a most instructive debate, although perhaps more instuctive for those of us who have the opportunity to savor it in the year 1984 than for those who happened to be listening in 1946. It casts a most ironical light on the subsequent events that are discussed by Timothy Brown in these pages.

In June, 1946, the United Nations Educational, Scientific, and Cultural Organization was still at the planning stage, but within a few weeks it would become a reality, ensconced in the former Majestic Hotel in Paris. Brought into existence as an educational adjunct to the United Nations during a brief period of post World War II utopianism, UNESCO was based on the unexamined assumption that international conflict came about because people across the globe didn't know very much about one another. Thus if only there could be exchanges of views--international gatherings, with everyone being paid per diem plus expenses, and gathering (it would turn out) at comfortable holiday resorts--why, then people would find out more about one another and the foundations of peace would be constructed in the hearts of men. As a result, wars would soon be a thing of the past.

Participants in the 1946 radio debate were Dr. Esther Brunauer, the U.S. representative on UNESCO's Preparatory Commission; Mr. Charles Thomson of the State Department; and Dr. Julian Huxley, the world-famous zoologist who would shortly become the first director general of UNESCO. At the outset Dr. Brunauer was asked to summarize UNESCO's purpose, bearing in mind (as the moderator sensibly cautioned) that the average listener in Butte or Shreveport would have no idea what UNESCO was, perhaps thinking that it sounds like "a cracker or a cookie--a cross between Uneeda and Nabisco."

Dr. Brunauer duly explained UNESCO as follows: "By the processes of learning, teaching, and thinking together, the peoples of the world will come infinitely nearer to establishing international peace and security."

"Can you tell us something about how this will be done," the moderator inquired, and Charles Thomson from the State Department responded:

"This will be done through exchanges of students, teachers, books, and so on. UNESCO is intended to work for a freer flow of ideas among nations by breaking down barriers of all sorts, and by using what we call the 'mass media'--the radio, press, and movies."

There ensued a brief discussion of illiteracy--that perennial top-of-the-list problem for intellectuals--and then Dr. Brunauer returned once again to the dreaded specter of all those barriers blocking the flow of information across the globe.

"But equally important," she said, if "UNESCO [is to be] a real agency for building the attitudes that will make for peace, [it must] break down the barriers to a free flow of information between countries. There are now, I am told, 53 restrictions on the distribution of films in Europe alone. It's up to UNESCO to free the press, movies, and radio of senseless restrictions."

"And on the positive side," added Thomson cheerfully, "to give the people of the world better channels of information from abroad."

"That's right," said Brunauer. "That means more cheap radio sets so that more people can listen to people of other countries; more freedom for newspapermen to gather and send news from any corner of the world; more movies of the type that will help to create better understanding throughout the world; cheaper books, more translations, more international magazines..."

"Dr. Huxley," the moderator interrupted, "do you attach the same degree of importance to mass communications?"

The great scientist, secular humanist, eugenicist, and world planner had been sitting in unaccustomed silence throughout these mounting effusions, but he bestirred himself to respond, not without a hint of disdain.

"I frankly admit, Mr. Fisher, that I have a lot to learn about the so-called 'mass media.'" The professor could almost be heard picking up the last two words with tweezers, and holding them at arm's length. "UNESCO is just starting to explore this field. The mass-media specialists should be patient with the scientists and professors, and the scientists and professors should not be condescending about the use of popular channels. But this is my conviction: The purpose of UNESCO is to build the defenses of peace in men's minds, and this can be done only by the effective use of mass communications to bring about <u>mutual understanding</u> among the peoples of the world."

* * *

That's the way it was. How do you like it now?

Poor Huxley lived long enough to see UNESCO steering way off the course that he and its other founders had envisioned for it, and in 1974 he even signed a petition protesting its anti-Israel posture. But he and the other radio broadcasters that day would surely not have expected that 30 years after their discussion, at its 1976 conference in Nairobi, UNESCO, by then under the leadership of the Senegalese Amadou Mahtar M'Bow, would be openly discussing and planning something called the New World Information Order: a thinly veiled attempt to <u>curtail</u> the free flow of information; to <u>reduce</u> the freedom of newspapermen to gather news; to <u>increase</u> the restraints on the transfer of data (including film) across national borders; to render <u>less</u> effective the use of mass communications.

How can this have come about in one generation? In his comments on the NBC broadcast, Julian Huxley did at one point seem to foresee the great obstacle to the attainment of UNESCO's goals--something that UNESCO since then has been powerless to do anything about. UNESCO was to be an organization of nations, whose national autonomy and sovereignty were totally unaffected by the creation of the UN body. UNESCO was (and is) simply a club which countries could join. It had no power within those countries.

Huxley, of course, saw nationalism as perhaps the world's overriding problem--a primitive emotion that gave rise to wars--and from a purely practical standpoint it certainly was a problem if UNESCO was to be anything more than a paper organization. In 1946, however, Huxley still entertained hopes that nationalism could be gradually eliminated; by, for example, permitting UNESCO officials "to free the textbooks of the world of nationalistic bias." But who on earth was about to give UNESCO officials that degree of latitude? Certainly not the new rulers of the increasing numbers of nations emerging across the world.

As Huxley feared, the post-war world has turned out to be one in which nationalism has been if anything stronger than it was before the United Nations came into existence. And the heads of the proliferating countries around the globe, while they have been only too happy to attend UNESCO meetings and denounce the United States for its sins, or denounce imperialism, or their next-door neighbors (while at the same time expecting the United States to pick up the bill, or the lion's share of it), have certainly not permitted the organization to do anything that would threaten their own personal power, or weaken their hold on the reins of government back home.

It turns out, of course, that information freely gathered and disseminated is as likely to cause conflict as it is harmony. This is especially the case when we consider such information in relation to the fortunes of national rulers who do not enjoy the consent of those they rule. It was the failure even to consider this possibility that was the principal error of UNESCO's founders and theoreticians. Accurate information about A transmitted to B does not necessarily increase B's love for A at all. A, for example, might be planning to do something unpleasant to B, and B won't like it if he finds out about it. Tyrants throughout history have regularly done unpleasant things to their subjects, and so we can readily see that such people would tend to take a dim view of investigative journalism. They might even be inhospitable to a free press. UNESCO's founders never seemed to consider this possibility. They seemed to be under the impression--curiously, in view of the recent memory of WWII--that everyone in the world was as well intentioned as they were.

An interesting story in a newspaper, while enjoyable for the reader, is very likely to discomfit the subject of the story. This is a fact of life, almost a truism, and virtually all journalists will agree with it. If a head of state has reason to believe that he does not enjoy popular support--and if he is not elected he probably has good reason to feel this way (benign despots, while theoretically possible, are hard to find)--then a relationship of mutual suspicion is likely to develop between him and his subjects. Secrecy will tend to envelop all his actions. The free flow of information is precisely what he will not relish, and will try to prevent. Crackdowns on press freedom will inevitably arise.

It is probably true that the greater the degree of control that a ruling elite exercises over the ordinary people, the greater will be the mutual suspicion between rulers and subjects, and the more restrictions will there be on the press. Thus in totalitarian countries (those with Communist governments) there will be no press freedom at all. In authoritarian countries (in which the rulers attempt to preserve their personal hold on power but do not try to supervise all aspects of their subjects' lives) there will very likely be frequent crackdowns on the press. In democratic countries the press will be free.

This does seem to correspond to the observed pattern, and it may also account for the fact that this glossary provides more examples of government action against the press in authoritarian states than in totalitarian ones. And there is, of course, a good reason for this. A government that owns the press and appoints its own officials to run it doesn't have to crack down on it. On the other hand, a government that tolerates free institutions but periodically applies the whip to them only draws attention to its disciplinary actions, and to its violations of human rights. For this reason many people have naively imagined that human rights abuses are worse in authoritarian than in totalitarian countries. In the same way, the naive observer might see prisoners strolling in a prison yard, then witness a heated street corner debate, and conclude that the former was the more tranquil milieu. It is only when a country is in the process of being subjugated by totalitarian rule that its coercive and violent nature is likely to be apparent to the casual observer. This appears now to be the case in Nicaragua, a country in which press freedom has been sharply curtailed in recent years. Mindful of world opinion, the Sandinistas still have not actually suppressed La Prensa, but they carefully censor it, achieving much the same effect.

The most important point to emerge from this work, as from an earlier one by Leonard R. Sussman,* the executive director of Freedom House, is that tyrants, rulers, autocrats, and dictators everywhere still feel obliged to pay lip service to freedom and democracy even as they stifle them. Even in communist countries, where party members exercise a level of control that is historically unprecedented, the rulers evidently feel obliged to practice a never-ending verbal deceit.

They call themselves "people's democratic republics," they flourish documents called "constitutions," in which the freedoms of the people are elaborately spelled out, and every few years they hold "elections." (In its external nomenclature, for example, the Soviet government might appear to have been modeled on the American: the Soviet "constitution" can only be amended, in theory, "by a two-thirds majority vote of both Houses.") Article 52 of the Cuban "constitution" mendaciously asserts that Cubans "have freedom of speech and of the press," adding, however, that this is "in keeping with the objectives of a socialist society." (The Article continues, more candidly and less promisingly: "Material conditions for the exercise of that right are provided by the fact that the press, radio, television, movies, and other organs of the mass media are state or social property and can never be private property.")

It is when non-democratic governments and the international organizations that they dominate (notably UNESCO) try to reconcile their unfree practices with their lip service to freedom that we enter the Orwellian realm. In many respects, obviously, George Orwell was too pessimistic when he wrote 1984. The world that he describes is

---

*Warning of A Bloodless Dialect: Glossary for International Communications, The Media Institute, 1983.

very much worse than anything that has since befallen the free world. (But here one must make a mental reservation about Cuba at least, and perhaps also Vietnam and Cambodia.)

Orwell did foresee, however, that tyrants would attempt to disguise their tyranny by altering the language: They would attempt to manipulate thought by manipulating words which, by repetition, might eventually come to mean their opposites: "war is peace," and so on.

Even so, a glance at Orwell's appendix to <u>1984</u>, "The Principles of Newspeak" ("the official language of Oceania"), shows that the rhetorical subterfuge of today's UNESCO workers is quite different from that envisioned by George Orwell. "In Newspeak," he writes, "euphony outweighed every consideration other than exactitude of meaning. Regularity of grammar was always sacrificed to it when it seemed necessary ... What was required above all for political purposes, were short clipped words of unmistakable meaning, which could be uttered rapidly and which roused the minimum of echoes in the speaker's mind."

UNESCOese isn't like that at all. UNESCO words tend to be long, extracted from social science or some other corner of academe, and of highly <u>mistakable</u> meaning. It is the sheer cloudiness of <u>UNESCO</u> syntax that at first baffles and ultimately drives off so many readers, and listeners. Who, for example, would know what the phrase "new world information order" itself meant, without being told? Each word individually is familiar enough. But their conjunction (three nouns strung together--an all-too-common bureaucratic formation) yields no clear meaning. To us, today, it does have a vaguely ominous ring, but that is only because various United Nations organizations have been minting similar phrases for over a decade now, and we have become gradually alerted to their illiberal implications.

But the main problem with UNESCO documents is that they are very nearly unreadable, in a way that Orwell did not foresee. As many people have complained, it is possible to read page after page of UNESCO-text without at any point having a very clear idea of what the writer is driving at; yet the text probably contains no technical terms. It is not the words themselves that are unfamiliar, but their meaning in the UNESCO context.

A look at Mr. Brown's list of words and phrases suggests that international bureaucrats have become adept at spraying out great clouds of abstract nouns which obscure our vision, defy all understanding, and encourage all but the most diligent verbal detectives to turn aside with a sigh of weariness and stupor: democratizing the press, communications infrastructures, developmental journalism, normative action, process news, new world information order--what can they all mean? In deciphering them for us, and setting them forth in plain English, Mr. Brown has performed a valuable service. As a result, let us hope, their continued use may be discouraged.

Tom Bethell
Washington, D.C.
September 1984

Chapter 1: Words & Phrases

1.1 Introduction

This part of the glossary explores how the advocates of a New World Information Order use language to mask their real intentions. The principal advocates are Communist and Third World countries. Their principal forum has been UNESCO (United Nations Educational, Scientific and Cultural Organization).

Cushrow Irani, a past chairman of the International Press Institute (IPI) and managing director of The Statesman in Calcutta, India, offers the following assessment of the real aims of the New World Information Order:

> They [NWIO advocates] will say they are doing this to fight against war and racial prejudice and to advance economic development. Their real objectives will be what they have always been, the enjoyment of political power without checks and balances, without accountability and, preferably, without end. (IPI Report, March 1980.)

The contrast between the words and actions of NWIO supporters in Communist and Third World countries quickly generates a sense of how they would implement their New Order. Their statements should not be taken at face value. The U.S.S.R. condemns censorship, yet maintains a bureaucracy of thousands of censors. Brazil touts its constitutional guarantee of free speech, yet makes it a crime to criticize the government. The Cameroons also has a constitutional guarantee of free speech, yet the government imposes fees and taxes that make it virtually impossible to publish a newspaper, unless you are a friend of the government.

In many cases, this glossary points up the discrepancies between the language used by governments at UNESCO, and the actions taken by those same governments.

One authority who read this manuscript before publication asked why there were not a larger number of direct quotes from UNESCO documents included in the text. Perhaps the following typical example of UNESCO prose will demonstrate why direct quotes are used relatively sparingly:

> Transformations in the structures of international communications, as a factor inherent in the conceptual foundations of international relations and of development, are frequently called for. It is argued that a world built on mutual understanding, acceptance of diversity, promotion of detente and coexistence, encouragement of trends toward real independence, not only needs but makes room for new, different patterns in international communication. If the conception of development as a linear, quantitative and exponential process, based on transfers of imported and frequently alienating technology, is beginning to be replaced by that of an endogenous qualitative process focused on man and his vital needs, aimed at eradicating inequalities and based on appropriate technologies which respect the cultural context and generate and foster the active participation of the populations concerned, then there can be no doubt that communication between people and nations will become different. (MacBride Report, page 38.)

It needs to be said here that not all the governments of developing countries--nor all socialist governments--inhibit their press or seek political domination in their own countries through manipulation and suppression of public information. And the appearance of one country or another in the glossary's examples should not be taken as a general condemnation of the government involved.

1.2 Words & Phrases--Entries

Access to Information

This phrase is usually used in the context of access to government information. For journalists in most of the developing and communist countries, "access to information" simply means being on the mailing list for government press releases. In such countries, access to information is something that governments control, and there are no Freedom of Information laws. Access to unauthorized information is often a crime for which foreign correspondents are deported, or local journalists are severely punished.

Access to information about the very workings of government is strictly controlled. China provides an example of how access to the most basic of government information is restricted--and the lengths to which governments will go to enforce that control.

> In March 1982, the editor of the China Finance and Trade News, L. Guangyi, was sentenced to five years in prison for leaking Chinese "state secrets" to foreign journalists. He had told foreigners the time, place and agenda of the 6th Full Assembly of the Communist Party Central Committee. That is equivalent to disclosing the sittings schedule for the U.S. Senate. (IPI Report, Dec. 1982.)

Information control is one of the basic tools of

the world's totalitarian regimes, be they of the left or the right. Walter Cronkite has described the control of information as "the primary tool for tyrants...The biggest thing since terror." Americans think of access to information as a corollary to freedom of the press--both essential prerequisites for good journalism and good government. But in most countries of the world legitimate access to information is severely limited or non-existent. So is a free press.

Access to Media

"Access to Media" means the ability of people, organizations and government agencies (not themselves in control of the media) to get information and opinion printed or broadcast. It does not refer to the proximity of a newspaper stand or ownership of a television. Many of the government members of UNESCO's club want to exercise total control over who and what has access to the media in their own countries. But these same governments are demanding unedited access to the media of the West, free-of-charge, for their propaganda pieces. This is part of their proposed New World Information Order. While UNESCO documents pay lip service to the concept of the public's access to all media, the principal access concern (as demonstrated in the most recent UNESCO Medium Term Plan) is governments' access to Western media. This demand has magically been elevated to the status of a "right"--a right which at the moment apparently exists nowhere except at UNESCO. But UNESCO is working to change that. (See discussions under "Right of Reply" and "Right of Correction," below.) What used to be considered a form of blackmail would be considered part of the new UNESCO panoply of rights.

During the Iranian hostage crisis NBC succumbed to demands made by the Iranians for access to the American airwaves. The Iranian material was televised unedited and without comment.

Access to Sources

As a matter of ideology, Marxist countries severely restrict journalists' access to both government and non-government sources. As a matter of pragmatism, many developing countries do the same thing. At the same time, these countries officially profess wholehearted support for numerous international agreements calling for free access by journalists to sources of information.

This apparent contradiction is explained away by a bit of legal sophistry. It is argued that the doctrine of National Sovereignty gives governments the right to control information flow within their own borders. Further, that right includes the power to decide who has access to which sources. Once a government exercises its legal right to decide which sources may be tapped, then (in compliance with international agreement) free access is allowed.

In October 1983, after two frustrating years, The Washington Post finally won permission for reporter William Claiborne to go to Angola. Once there, he asked for interviews with several government officials. None was granted--"It is not on the program," he was informed. Apparently the only thing that was on the program was a tribute to the late Agostinho Neto--one of the founders of the Marxist state.

On the same Angola trip, two French reporters wanted to interview some nuns. The reporters snuck out of their hotel, and after skulking down dark alleys and back streets, they finally found the Roman Catholic mission. Alas, to no avail. Angolan security nabbed them. And threatened to throw all visiting journalists out of the country immediately if any further attempt were made to talk to the nuns. It was no idle threat. At the time of the incident, there were no accredited Western journalists based in Angola. The last Agence France-Presse reporter was expelled in April 1983 for "sensationalist, alarming and distorted" reporting. (The Washington Post, Oct. 8, 1983.)

The U.S.S.R. government regularly refuses journalists permission to go farther than 40 miles from downtown Moscow, and Zimbabwe requires a pass wrapped in red tape for newsmen to venture more than 25 miles from Harare or Bulawayo. (World Press Freedom Review, 1982.)

Advertising

At UNESCO, advertising is considered one of the most corrupting influences of colonialism and economic imperialism. As the MacBride Report states (page 111):

> Hence, some developing countries depend for the financing and indeed the existence of their broadcasting systems, not merely on advertising, but on imported advertising... seen by many as a threat to the cultural identity and self-realization of many developing countries: it brings to many people alien ethical values; it may deviate consumer demands in developing countries to areas which can inhibit development priorities; it affects and can often deform ways of life and lifestyles. Moreover, the threat to withdraw advertising--by private interests or by a government--can jeopardize press freedom.

When domestic government advertising is at issue, it seems to be considered a legitimate means of access to the people. But government advertising can also be an extremely valuable tool for bending privately owned media to the government's will. In most developing countries, the bulk of the local media's revenues come from advertising, employment classifieds and public notices of the government and government-owned enterprises. In Mexico, the government controls 75 percent of the economy, including supermarkets and service stations. A threatened or actual boycott can work wonders on an antagonistic newspaper's editorial policy.

> Two newspapers and a privately owned news agency that were critical of the Mexican government were crippled when the government withdrew its advertising accounts in December 1982. Up to 50 percent of all ads in Mexican papers and magazines are paid for by the government. (IPI Report, April 1983.)

Private-sector advertising frightens Third World governments that are not already committed to a socialist system. One of their fears is that too much exposure to Western lifestyles through ads will raise expectations that the government will not be able to meet, with resulting unrest.

> In 1981 Indonesian President Suharto banned all non-government advertisements on TV, claiming the ads promoted "wasteful consumerism," raised "unrealizeable expectations," caused "rural dissatisfaction," and encouraged further unwanted migration to the cities. (Index on Censorship, Oct. 1982.)

Another fear is that control over a financially independent domestic media will be more difficult to maintain. The print and broadcast media in the

United States are almost completely dependent on private advertising revenue, and completely inde-pendent of a government which they often criti-cize. Virtually all radio and television broadcasting facilities in developing countries are state-owned. Very few allow private advertisements (See "Information Infrastructure," below.)

UNESCO's MacBride Commission Report not only displayed a bias against private ownership of communications media, it blithely referred to the "problems created in a society by advertising," without stopping to analyze what, if any, problems in fact exist. The report encouraged governments to establish their own communications systems and "reduce the negative effects of the influences of market and commercial considerations." (page 260)

Alternative Media

The Third World has taken a Western phrase with good connotations and used it to describe something exactly opposite to the original meaning. The traditional Western concept of "alternative media" encompasses two distinct types of publications: (a) in countries with a free press "alternative media" are those that are not considered "mainstream" (e.g. The Village Voice), and (b) in countries lacking a free press, the phrase "alternative media" usually refers to "Samizdat" (underground publications that are not under government control). In developing countries, the phrase "alternative media" is often used to describe media owned or controlled by the governments, and which promulgate uncritical development news and government press releases. This includes more than 100 national and regional state-run news agencies, many of which are funded by money from UNESCO's International Program for the Development of Communication (IPDC). "Alternative" here means

9

alternative to the free Western media, which are represented by AP, Reuters, etc. This is a classic example of the perversion of language at UNESCO. True alternative media don't fare well in most communist and developing countries.

> In Poland, possession of the Samizdat of Solidarity was declared a crime punishable by three to five years in prison, after the government shut down 400 Solidarity newspapers with a circulation of 1.5 million. (<u>World Press Freedom Review</u>, 1982.)

> In 1982 Suriname's government closed all non-government radio stations. Two privately owned radio stations and one newspaper were set ablaze and firemen were instructed by government officials to let the fire burn. The one remaining newspaper in Suriname is subject to rigid government control of its content. (<u>The Washington Post</u>, Oct. 13, 1983.)

Censorship

In UNESCO documents censorship is either condemned or denied. Nevertheless, censorship is practiced by the governments of three out of every four countries in the world, according to a recent Freedom House study. Most developing and socialist countries lack a free press. As discussed elsewhere (see "Role of the Media" and "Freedom of the Press," below) implementation of the New World Information Order would hand governments a carte blanche for censorship of the international press, in addition to justifying the muzzling of their domestic media.

> Red China banned sales of the September 22, 1983 issue of <u>Time</u> magazine. The cover story was titled "Banishing Mao's Ghost," and author

Theodore White had speculated that at the end Mao was "with almost no doubt, insane." (The Washington Post, Sept. 23, 1983.) According to Curtis Prendergast, of Time magazine, "practically every week we find ourselves banned outright or having stories excised out of the magazine in one country or another." Other examples: Because of a 400-word story on Shiite Muslims, one issue was banned in Pakistan and the story was cut out of the magazine in India; A full-page story ("Lust City in the Far East") describing sex tours to Bangkok got Time banned in Thailand. (Communications in a Changing World, The Media Institute.)

In 1983 Indonesian newspapers were reporting the summary executions of hundreds of known and suspected criminals. The government ordered such reports to stop. But two weeks later, there was much press ballyhoo by the official press agency, Antara, when President Suharto released 3,198 prisoners and reduced the sentences of 14,000 others in celebration of the Indonesian national holiday. (The Washington Post, Aug. 5 and 18, 1983.)

Socialist countries take a different view of censorship than we in the West do, and what they can't explain, they deny.

Sergei Losev of Tass, the Russian delegate to UNESCO's MacBride Commission (see separate entry), wrote flatly that there is no censorship in the USSR. This, in spite of the fact that Russia's Central Board for the Safeguarding of State Secrets in the Press employs 70,000 censors and provides them with a 300-page index of information that can't be published without government consent--e.g., no mention of dissidents except to report their court sentences; at one point in the '70s, use of the word "vodka" was banned completely. (Index on Censorship, March 1982.) According to our Russian friend, censorship implies withholding information from the people, but in socialist countries, the government is the people. Therefore it is impossible for that situation to arise. Besides, he said, censorship is unnecessary because all opposition to the Soviet government ceased in the 1920s.

UNESCO, it should be noted, denies that its New World Information Order initiatives will lead to censorship. UNESCO accuses those who say otherwise of plotting unjustly against the organization:

There is a well-orchestrated crusade under way within some media which seeks to make UNESCO the hub of a sinister machination against press freedom and the nerve center of a "censorship operation at a world level." Supporting this war machine there is a manichean argumentation [sic] as well as a battery of gratuitous affirmations and defamatory accusations. (UNESCO press release, March 1982.)

Code of Ethics

Proponents of the New World Information Order speak often of the need for a Code of Ethics for international journalists. This at first blush does not seem to be too stringent a requirement. After all, American journalists are expected to comply with a Code of Ethics set out by The Society of Professional Journalists (Sigma Delta Chi) that runs to about 800 words and speaks to Responsibility, Freedom of the Press, Accuracy and Objectivity, and Fair Play. However, the NWIO proposal is misleading. What is sought is in fact a Code of Conduct, not Ethics. And the conduct would be enforceable by a body comprised of governments. The Code would be set up in conjunction with a licensing scheme. Journalists found not to act properly, in the NWIO context, would be stripped of their licenses and liable to jail sentences. (See "Licensing of Journalists," below.) Part of any proposed NWIO code would be a requirement that foreign journalists respect the press laws of each individual country and work to further the National Communications Policies of each country. Most of the countries in the world consider the press a tool of the government and an instrument for furthering state policy. In practical terms, such an arrangement would mean that any reporter who writes an unflattering truth about a government could be punished. A Code of Ethics as envisioned by NWIO supporters is in reality an attempt to get Western journalists to agree in principle to UNESCO's arguments. It could be carved as the epitaph on the tombstone of a free press. UNESCO is not the only UN organization to lobby for such codes of conduct. The United Nations Commission on Transnational Corporations (see separate entry) has drafted a Code and is trying to see it implemented.

Collaboration of Various Groups and Professional Communicators

For "collaboration," read "coercion." This is another euphemism for government control of the press. The essence of the NWIO's concept of collaboration is for journalists and media outlets to work within the framework of each country's National Communication Policy. And if a member of the press won't work at the government's direction, then that member won't be able to work at all.
UNESCO's MacBride Commission Recommendation #58 included the following:

Effective legal measures should be designed

to:...(b) circumscribe the action of transnationals by requiring them to comply with specific criteria and conditions defined by national legislation and development policies.

Translation: Unless foreign journalists and news services report what Third World governments tell them to report, they should be thrown in jail, fined or thrown out of the country.

Commercialization of Communications

Advocates of the New World Information Order object to the commercialization of communications as if it were a loss of virtue--and infinitely worse than the commercialization of Christmas. Western commercial news and entertainment programming is seen as a threat to one of UNESCO's newly minted rights--the Right to Cultural Identity (see separate entry). Pervasive Western ads and TV programs are said to promote consumerism. And, because the world's mass media are dominated by the products of alien Western society, Third World governments claim they are concerned about the erosion of their national cultures. Experts with a great deal of experience in the field of Third World communications suggest, however, that more practical reasons underlie the UNESCO antipathy to advertising: (1) Dissatisfaction and political restiveness can develop from constant exposure to the apparently unattainable standard of living enjoyed in developed Western countries; and (2) Advertising revenues can provide a measure of financial independence for the media, thus removing, or reducing the effectiveness of, one lever of government control. (See also "Advertising," above.)

The Indian government imposes an arbitrary upper limit of 40 percent on the amount of advertising allowed in newspapers. (C. Irani,

The Statesman, in <u>Communications in a Changing World</u>, The Media Institute.)

The Indian restriction applies to domestic advertising. Such actions undercut somewhat the arguments against commercialization which focus on the Western influence.

Communications

In 1981 Cushrow Irani, a prominent Indian journalist and editor, wrote that at UNESCO:

> For many years now there has been a deliberate confusion between communications and information...Communications are simply the channel or the medium. Information is what you feed into the channel or medium.

From the point of view of UNESCO and Second and Third World members, this confusion has borne fruit. They have declared state control of "communications" essential for development. By deliberately confusing the concepts of content and medium, they have justified state control of the contents of messages in the telecommunications and broadcasting fields, not just regulation of the means of transmission. Thus, the original UNESCO proposals for "national communications policies" have been transformed. In many cases, national communications policies have become national information policies--systems of information control and censorship.

Communications Infrastructures

In the usual parlance of the West, "communications infrastructure" is a phrase used to describe the physical plant and organizational structure of the communications industry. In UNESCOese the phrase describes a system of government controls over all phases and aspects of communications technologies and the media, from printing presses to journalism schools to satellites to radio transmitters to newsprint to journalists themselves.

The 1976 UNESCO agenda called for members "to consider the establishment of governmental administrative, technical, research and training infrastructures" to put national communications policies into effect.

Correct and Factual Information

This is one of the best examples of how UNESCO members redefine words to subvert their original meaning, and then use them for political and ideological purposes. In the West, "correct and factual information" is generally assumed to have some basis in objective fact, and relate closely to the truth. The source of information has no bearing on its correct and factual nature. Not so in the world of the Third World majority around UNESCO. Many "nonaligned" nations have joined the Nonaligned Press Agencies Pool (NANAP) which is touted as an objective alternative news source to the biased Western "transnationals" (news services). Thus it masquerades as a source of correct and factual information about member countries. This is belied by the Constitution of NANAP: Statements made by any government news agency about its own country must be regarded as "correct and factual," and such reports must be relayed by the press pool in unedited and unaltered form.

Democratizing the Press

When communist and developing countries speak of

democratizing the press, they do not mean giving more control or media access to the citizenry. They mean increasing government control over the media. Since governments are the surrogates of the people as a collective, it is argued, government control is in fact democratization.

UNESCO's concept of "democracy" owes more to the U.S.S.R. than to the U.S.A., as the MacBride Report makes clear. Recommendation #53 on Democratization of Communication reads as follows:

> The media should contribute to promoting the just cause of peoples struggling for freedom and independence and their right to live in peace and equality without foreign interference. This is especially important for all oppressed peoples who, while struggling against colonialism, religious and racial discrimination, are deprived of opportunity to make their voices heard within their own countries. (page 265)

> Sudan democratized its press in 1970 by nationalizing all outlets. Peru's government declared it was democratizing the press by taking control of the six major papers in 1974. Such democratization has taken place all over the world since the early 70s. In Africa as early as 1976, 51 of the 71 African dailies were either owned by the governments or parties in power in the countries. And, as reported by the MacBride Commission, all national broadcasting systems in Africa are either owned and operated directly by governments or indirectly, as in Ghana, Malawi, Mauritius and Nigeria where "nominal" control is exercised by a government-owned corporation. (page 102)

Developmental Journalism

Developmental journalism is newsgathering and

publication calculated to assist developing countries in their growth, politically, culturally and economically, according to advocates of the New World Information Order. As the MacBride Report recognizes:

> The current world debate on communication is inevitably political, because the anxieties, the aims and the arguments have a primarily political character.

The term "development" has undergone a radical redefinition since the '60s when it was assumed to mean economic development (and probably still is, by most Westerners). Western countries may not accept the new meaning, but Third World countries see the goal of development as "profound and widespread social transformation." Development is a political goal as much as an economic one.

Behind the demands for a change in Western news coverage is a desire to use the Western media as a political tool. To justify their demands, they claim (with precious little evidence) that the Western media do not help "development," but actually inhibit it. According to a member of the MacBride Commission:

> The news brought from the developing countries is usually only about exceptional or dramatic events, clashes, crises of various sorts, or about events which are important in connection with the exploitation of their wealth--not to mention the biased and tendentious reports which reflect specific foreign interests or remnants of colonialist attitudes.

Free and Balanced Flow of Information

NWIO advocates claim that the free flow of information concept (established by the Universal Declaration of Human Rights) has in fact led to a one-way flow of information from the West to the developing world. To cure this lack of balance in information flow and force the flow of more information back to the West, the NWIO would throw out the concept of free flow and replace it with the concept of "free and balanced flow."

The MacBride Commission Report cites as evidence of this "striking imbalance" the following:

> AP sends out on its general world wire service to Asia from New York an average of 90,000 words daily. In return Asia files 19,000 words to New York for worldwide distribution. UPI's general news wire out of New York to Asia totals some 100,000 words and the file from all points in Asia to New York varies between 40,000 to 45,000 daily...The flow of news is uneven in that a lot more is sent from London or New York to Asia than the other way around.

The fact that the feed from the West carries news of the rest of the entire world to Asia, while the Asia return feed only carries Asian items is cavalierly ignored.

This "free and balanced" formulation is put forward as a modification to "free flow" that will ensure a truly free flow of information between the developed and developing world. But an examination of some of the comments of NWIO supporters makes it clear that this is just one step in a strategy to eliminate free flow altogether. The request for "balance" appears reasonable, on its face. But, like many UNESCO ideas that have a pleasing surface appearance, it hides a much darker underside. The ultimate goal is to replace the international flood of free-flowing information with carefully regulated trickles. And the socialist and authoritarian governments of the world will have their hands on the taps. Two of the more difficult aspects of achieving a balanced information flow are: (1) deciding what constitutes a balance, and (2) enforcing that decision.

According to MacBride Commission member Bogdan Osolnik:

> This concept represents an advance from the principle of unlimited freedom of the international flow of information--which led to a predominantly one-way flow and had other consequences...In my opinion the formula "free and balanced flow" is inadequate for several reasons. Above all, it is not clear enough. What does the qualification "balanced" flow mean? Is it a question of quantitative balance or balance with regard to content? What are the criteria in this regard and in particular: how can this balance be achieved and what measures should be taken and who is to intervene when the given conditions in themselves do not permit balance?

UNESCO's Second and Third World governments have a simple solution--let their individual governments control the flow of international information. Decisions about who gets what information will be made and enforced according to their own National Communication Policies. That means using the media as a tool for the furtherance of government policy and power. All of this apparently "ivory-tower" kind of discussion about various phrases and formulations is not conducted in a vacuum.

> Perhaps the clearest example this year of a direct causal link between debates at UNESCO and actions in the real world is the case of Malaysia. Its government in June 1983 approved a plan to make the government-dominated news agency, Bernama, the sole distributor in Malaysia of all news entering or leaving the country...Bernama is reported to have conceded that it already practices self-censorship and

omits news reports on instruction from government officials. Information Minister Adib Adam provided a rationale often heard at UNESCO: The takeover, he said, will be "an exercise in national sovereignty." The application of government controls, he said further, "will help correct the imbalance in the flow" of information between the developing and developed countries...Clearly [Malaysia] is developing a "national communications policy"--an objective repeatedly urged at UNESCO --and such centralized policies lead rather naturally to central control of news media. (Excerpt from Freedom House's *Freedom in the World 1983-1984*, p. 58.)

To some extent the NWIO forces have already been successful in eroding the "free flow" idea. A 1978 consensus resolution of the Special Political Committee of the UN General Assembly contained the following compromise language approved by a grudging U.S.: "Free Flow and a Wider and Better Balanced Dissemination of Information."

Freedom of Information

The Western concept of Freedom of Information doesn't seem to exist in the current NWIO lexicon. (See discussion of "Access to Information," above.) In the MacBride Report, Freedom of Information is described as a stage in the evolutionary development of the debate over communications:

> Thus the problems of communication--successively presented as freedom of the press, freedom of information and right to information--have become more and more political, economic and social in character. (page 20)

When the Report discusses freedom of information in a current context, the phrase passes through a blizzard of verbiage to emerge somehow as a synonym for the concept of free flow of information between countries--quite a different meaning from the original concept of access to government information by the governed:

> Freedom of information is of major concern to everyone; a generous aspiration which, however, as a doctrine has been misapplied and narrowly interpreted and for which all necessary conditions for its genuine implementation on both the national and world level have yet to be created. These aspects have drawn our particular attention and we feel they may be equally salient for all others interested in communication development and democratization. Hence, we do not feel that frank recognition of an imbalance in information flows is a threat to freedom of information. On the contrary, if the causes of the imbalance disappear, many arguments for restricting the free flow of information will also disappear. (page 144)

Freedom of the Press

Freedom of the press simply does not exist in most countries of the world.

> Governments in three-fourths of the world have a significant or dominant voice in determining what does and what does not appear in the media. This definition of control does not include regulation such as that practiced by the FCC: it means control over newspaper or broadcast content...In only one-fourth of the countries are both the print and broadcast media generally free. (Freedom House report, Freedom in the World 1983-1984, p. 55.)

Where press freedoms do exist, they are under attack, as a continual barrage of news stories attests. The print media in Nigeria were described as "generally free" in Freedom in the World 1983-1984. No longer.

On April 18, 1984, The Washington Post reported:

> Nigeria's government published a restrictive press law giving it the power to close down newspapers and radio stations and jail journalists.

And UNESCO is right there, cheering on the attackers. Leonard Sussman, Executive Director of Freedom House, writes about "fears that UNESCO has been a clearinghouse, perhaps the coordinator, of carefully conceived proposals to alter the content of the worldwide news flow." And Sussman states that "UNESCO indirectly sustains the trend toward licensing as well as other forms of government influence over press content." In UNESCO documents, one rarely sees the phrase Freedom of the Press without the word "responsibility" lurking somewhere nearby. Freedom and responsibility do go together. But not the type of responsibility that a lot of UNESCO members have in mind. They want the press to be responsible to the government and under government control, allegedly to further the country's development goals. What it comes down to is government-controlled press--and that makes a mockery of the "fredom" part of "freedom and responsibility." (See "Responsibility of the Press," below.) To get an appreciation of how differently others may see the issue of press freedom, consider the following:

> In a submission to the MacBride Commission, the Soviet bloc's International Organization of Journalists claimed that to Western journalists "Freedom of the Press" meant "Freedom to Wage Cold War."

(Hypocrisy has its place in any discussion of freedom of the press.)

In August 1980 the government of South Korea closed 172 periodicals for printing material that was "corrupt, lewd and vulgar, causing social decay and juvenile delinquency." One of the allegedly disgusting publications was the intellectual weekly, <u>Deep-Rooted Trees</u>, put out by the <u>Encyclopaedia Britannica</u>. The official notice declared that the government "will continue to guarantee freedom of the press in accordance with the constitution." (<u>World Press Freedom Review</u>, 1980.)

Free Flow of Ideas by Word and Image

This phrase is contained in Article I of UNESCO's constitution. It was intended to encourage information transfer between countries, unhindered by government censors and monopolistic businesses. This is the source of one of the major friction points in the whole NWIO debate--the concept of "free flow of information." (See discussion of "Free Flow of Information," below.)

Free Flow of Information

This concept has been the basis of international information law and practice since the principle of Free Flow of Ideas by Word and Image was adopted by the UN and its agencies shortly after World War II. It has been under more or less continual attack ever since adopted, even though it is enshrined in the Universal Declaration of Human Rights. Under the free flow of information concept, governments must not interfere with the activities of journalists in the collection, creation or publication of news; not engage in censorship within their borders; nor inhibit the transmission of news from country to country. Communist countries argue that "free flow" interferes with a country's sovereignty and may be abridged by a government whenever it chooses. Developing countries claim they want to jettison the concept because free flow is in fact a one-way flow, from the developed world to the developing world. The reality is that Second and Third World governments dislike the free flow of information because it is not compatible with strict government control over the media. One of the major aspects of the NWIO is rejection of "free flow."

Free flow of information "perpetuates colonialism, economic exploitation, humiliation" and is a "deliberate denial of cultural opportunity," according to Vidya Charan Shukla, president of the 1976 New Delhi Conference of the Nonaligned Press Agencies Pool (NANAP). "The 'free' flow of information, which was chanted in a chorus, aimed to enable all countries in name, but only the powerful countries in reality, to pump their information into all the regions of the world without let or hindrance."

The Cuban delegate to the Acapulco UNESCO conference said, "Free flow is the enemy of the New World Information Order."

UNESCO was a fervent supporter of the free flow concept until 1976, when there was a "shift in emphasis in the Organization's communication program" (according to a UNESCO pamphlet titled, paradoxically, "For the Free Flow of Ideas"). At that point UNESCO and its Director General threw themselves into the fray on the side of the "New World Information Order" with the fervor reserved only for recent converts. UNESCO is now officially opposed to continuation of the free flow doctrine. (See "Free and Balanced Flow of Information," above.)

Harnessing the Power of Communication

This is one of the most graphic of UNESCO's phrases describing a system of government control over communications and the press. Attempts have been made to insert the phrase into formal UNESCO resolutions, but Western representatives have been successful in keeping it out. UNESCO's Director General M'Bow wants the press to be harnessed by governments and used as a beast of burden to further political ends. The bit placed in the press' mouth would serve as restraint, guide and gag.

Information

In UNESCOese, the definition of the word "information" varies. It covers a great deal and seems like an infinitely expandable mantle as governments and UNESCO seek to bring more and more activities under government control. Information includes, among other things, print and broadcast news; computer data; books; mail; telephone transmissions; scientific, technical, financial and commercial data; magazines; commercial films; TV and radio entertainment programs; and even music.

> Between 1980 and 1983, Jordan sentenced several people to up to ten years in prison because they were caught with cassette tapes of certain Egyptian and Iraqi singing stars. And in Saudi Arabia, Oman and Bahrain, citizens have been jailed and foreign nationals thrown out of the country for the same offense. (IPI Report, Feb. 1983.)

For a discussion of how UNESCO blurs the concept of information to mean "communication," thus including the technology of transmission as well as what is transmitted, see the separate entry "Communications."

Information Gap

At UNESCO this phrase was originally used to

describe the discrepancy between the amount of information available to the citizens of developing countries and the amount of information available to those in the developed nations.

In 1957 UNESCO published a report on the world's "information famine" showing that two billion people, inhabitants of more than 100 countries, "lacked even minimum access to information and to the general education which mass media can provide." "Minimum access" was defined (per 100 people) as being "10 copies of a daily newspaper, five radio sets, two cinema seats and two television receivers."

In one background paper written in 1979 for the MacBride Commission the phrase "information gap" was being used to describe the difference in <u>quality</u> of information available to people in developing countries, rather than the quantity. The people in almost all developing countries may now have some form of mass communications infrastructure and more than minimum access to information, but that information is about the West and not about the developing world. The New World Information Order is supposed to close that gap to some extent. And one way of doing it, according to NWIO advocates, is through National Communications Policies--or to say it another way--government control over the mass media and all the news and information printed or broadcast by those media. This approach results in a third type of "information gap." That is, a gap between what the government knows and what it will allow the people to know. Communist governments already have this system.

> Poland's Central Office of Press Publications and Spectacles Control (COPPSC) lists subjects which the media are forbidden to report on. Excerpts from the COPPSC Directives demonstrate the kinds of things which fall into Poland's information gap. Some examples are: (1) information on increasing pollution of

rivers flowing from Czechoslovakia; (2) the "rise of alcoholism in Poland;" (3) "all criticism of income and social policies, including wage claims;" (4) the "annual consumption of coffee in Poland...in order to prevent the disclosure of our coffee re-exportation;" (5) "In reports about the Polish exhibition in Moscow, excessive emphasis on the successes of a particular exhibitor should be avoided, because this could suggest that some Polish products created a furor in Moscow and were not previously known on the Soviet market." (MacBride Commission Background Paper #52 by Frank Giles, Deputy Editor of London's <u>The Sunday Times</u>.)

Many developing countries would like to see that same type of information gap in their countries.

In spite of Brazil's constitutionally guaranteed right of free speech, it is a crime punishable by six months to two years in prison to publish true facts which might cause "antagonism between the people and the authorities." (Giles, see above.)

Ghanian law makes publishing "rumours" a punishable offense. The government is the source of "fact" and anything else falls into the information gap labeled "rumour." Although the press in other countries carried extensive reports of a 1977 abortive coup attempt in Ghana, it received no mention whatever in the Ghanian press. (Giles, see above.)

Information Infrastructure

UNESCO Director General M'Bow has used the phrase "information infrastructure" to describe systems of government control over news and information. (See also "Communication Infrastructure," above; and "Progressive Incorporation of Communications Technology," below.) This is a far cry from its original meaning. The phrase is used in the West to describe either the corporate organization of the industry or the communications hardware facilities at the disposal of the industry. Time magazine has accused UNESCO of emptying Western concepts of their meaning. But UNESCO actually goes further than that. The empty vessels of words are refilled with new meanings. When funds are allocated by the International Program for the Development of Communications (see separate entry) or UNESCO for improving the communications infrastructures of developing countries, the money is not destined to help the nations' private sector economies or businesses (with one small exception--Freedom in the World 1983-1984 reports that in 1983 a small IPDC grant was made to an independent newspaper in Botswana to establish the principle that aid could be given to non-governmental media). Virtually all the money is spent for government-owned news agencies and broadcasting facilities, and government-run training schools for journalists that turn out graduates more akin to press agents than newsmen.

As of February 1983, ownership of radio and television stations in the developing countries of the Middle East was as follows: ALGERIA--13 radio and 6 TV controlled by a state-owned and operated corporation. BAHRAIN--2 radio and 1 TV operated by state-owned agencies. EGYPT--30 radio and 1 TV government-owned and operated. IRAQ--2 radio and 8 TV controlled by the Ministry of Information. JORDAN--1 radio and 1 TV run by state corporations controlled by the Ministry of Communications. KUWAIT--1 radio and 1 TV run by state-owned Kuwait Broadcasting Service and Television of Kuwait. LEBANON--11 radio and 3 TV owned by the government. LIBYA--15 radio and 13 TV run by the government's Secretariat of Information. OMAN--2 radio and 2 TV government-owned and operated. QATAR--2 radio and 2 TV owned and run by the Ministry of Information. SAUDI ARABIA--3 radio and 11 TV controlled by government's Saudi Arabian Broadcasting Service; 1 radio and 1 TV owned and run by ARAMCO oil company with service restricted to ARAMCO employees. SUDAN--1 radio and 1 TV owned and run by Departments of the Ministry of Information and Culture. SYRIA--6 radio and 5 TV run by the state-owned Syrian Broadcasting and Television Corporation. TUNISIA--4 radio and 2 TV run by a corporation owned by the Ministry of Information and Culture. UNITED ARAB EMIRATES--4 radio and 2 TV state-owned and operated. YEMAN ARAB REPUBLIC--3 radio and 1 TV state-owned and operated. (World Press Encyclopedia and IPI Report.)

In 1976 a formal resolution of the UNESCO General Conference encouraged all states to "take all necessary steps, including legislative measures" to establish government control of "information media."

International Information Law

At the moment there is very little "law" in the international communications area. What little law there is, is not particularly relevant to present-day circumstances. It has been far outstripped by technological advances. This whole area is in a state of flux and development. Most international law derives from custom and general agreement among nations. Because virtually every country in the world belongs to UNESCO, its policies and pronouncements have the potential of developing into international law. That is one of the major reasons why the proposed New World

Information Order should be so frightening to the West.

Journalistic Pluralism

Journalistic Pluralism, as touted at UNESCO, is the theory of the positive development of multiple news sources to improve the quality, quantity and flow of news, to and from all countries of the world. In practice, this means the development of alternatives to the Western news agencies--alternatives in the form of socialist and Third World news agencies and reporters under the thumbs of governments. Pluralism is in effect simply the replacement of representatives of a free press with members of a controlled press.

> Zimbabwe received unfavorable coverage in the Western press over its political repression and reports of more than 1,000 dissident supporters being slaughtered by the Army. Unhappy with the coverage, particularly from British reporters, Zimbabwe expelled some journalists, and announced that it was signing contracts with Soviet, East German and Bulgarian news agencies--agencies which provided more satisfactory coverage of the country. (The Washington Post, Aug. 2, 1983.)

The governments of most Third World countries do not want to see more news about themselves; they want to see more positive news about themselves. They want image builders writing the news, not reporters.

> "There are good journalists and bad journalists," said Joaquin Espirito, a reporter for the state-operated Journal of Angola, succinctly summing up his government's policy. "We only allow the good ones to come to Angola." (The Washington Post, Oct. 8, 1983.)

Licensing of Journalists

UNESCO's Communist and Third World majority wants to license foreign journalists so they can be given government "protection"--the kind of protection that Al Capone used to offer. Each year hundreds of journalists are abducted, tortured, jailed or murdered. But (according to Amnesty International, which documented 300 cases in 1982) most of the abducting, torturing, jailing and killing is done by governments. By and large these are the same governments pushing the licensing and protection scheme. One of the conditions for keeping a journalist's license would, of course, be continued compliance with a Code of Ethics. Such an arrangement would give governments effective control over what foreign journalists do and, most importantly, what they write.

At least eight Latin American countries already require their local newspeople to obtain licenses. And Latin America has the worst record for murdered and "disappeared" journalists. Countries with licensing systems are: Nicaragua, Cuba, Chile, Venezuela, Colombia, Panama, Haiti and Costa Rica. Costa Rica also forces applicants for a journalist's license to "graduate" from a government-run course. (Freedom in the World 1983-1984.)

National Communications Policies

The phrase "National Communications Policies," in the UNESCO context, describes a system of government dominance and control--a tool for the perpetuation and political aggrandizement of existing regimes. The purpose of National Communications Policies is stated to be furthering the goals of "development" through use of modern communications. But "communications" at UNESCO is taken to include the mass media and news organizations, and "development" means the furthering of governments' political and social goals, not just economic development. (See separate entry, "Developmental Journalism," above.)

The UNESCO agenda as far back as 1976 declared "a national communications policy is necessary in order to help safeguard national sovereignty." At that time UNESCO Director General M'Bow described national communications policies as "coherent sets of principles and norms designed to act as general guidelines for communications organs and institutions."

The aim is to "harness the media" and ensure its "commitment to development." In the 1960s, many authoritarian governments in the Third World were saying, in effect, "We want a free press like the West, but that will have to come later. Our countries are too vulnerable right now to let the media play that role." Now, in many cases, these authoritarian governments and others who have come along since are happy with their control over the media and don't want a free press after all. Authoritarian Third World governments start from the premise that collective rights are generally more important than individual rights. If this turning upside down of one of Western society's cornerstones is accepted, then simple logic dictates that the media exist primarily for the benefit of the collective (government), and not for individuals. All else follows, and the media's role becomes clear in the context of national communications policies.

National News Agencies

According to the governments of Third World and communist countries, these organizations provide more accurate, balanced and timely news about their countries. And they counter the "pernicious effects" of Western wire service coverage. There are now about 105 of these agencies (Freedom in the World 1983-1984). They generally have the sole right to distribute news inside their countries (See "News Monopolies," below), and generally function as an arm of the government, to be used for political purposes. UNESCO and the International Program for the Development of Communications have provided millions of dollars to help set up many of these agencies.

Articles written by Gerald Long, managing director of Reuters, and Leonard Marks of the World Press Freedom Committee call National News Agencies "instruments of national propaganda" that issue "self-congratulatory press releases prepared by information ministries"--not news reports.

Nationalization of Communications Technology

(See "Democratizing the Press.")

News

The concept of news in the West encompasses reports of occurrences which are novel, interesting, important. It is expected that reporters and news outlets will provide facts as objectively as humanly possible and will be as fair as possible in their coverage, uncowed by fear or favor of government, or anyone else. Great reliance is placed on the ability of journalists to dig out the news, their news judgment in deciding what news to report and their integrity in making these decisions. In most of the communist and developing world, governments control the news media and government officals decide what is and isn't news. These are the same governments pushing for the adoption of the New World Information Order, so they can have the kind of control over international news that they currently enjoy regarding domestic news.

The report of the 1968 Russian invasion of Czechoslovakia was limited to only one or two paragraphs in the Russian press. (F. Giles, of the Sunday Times, in a paper for the MacBride Commission.)

Four days after Lech Walesa's 1983 Nobel Peace Prize was announced in Sweden, the Soviet government newspaper Izvestia described Walesa as a "low-grade hustler" who became a millionaire while purportedly waging a disinterested struggle for workers' rights in Poland. Izvestia made no mention of Walesa's Nobel Prize. It was not considered "news." When word of Walesa's honor became widespread, Pravda was forced to acknowledge it. But in doing so, referred to Walesa in unflattering terms and claimed the award was a propaganda ploy by the West. (The Washington Post, Oct. 8, 1983.)

Consider a Soviet official's criteria for deciding what is and isn't news. In 1979, Bogdan Osolnik, a member of the MacBride Commission, wrote a paper for the Commission condemning the following definition of news:

> Primarily that which is unusual, exceptional, alarming or sensational--anything which can be profitably sold on the "news market."

News Monopoly

Breaking the alleged "news monopoly" of the Western news agencies is a principal rallying cry of NWIO supporters, who claim that AP, UPI, Reuters and Agence France-Presse:

> have, by reason of their equipment and capital, acquired a position of strength which probably enables them to offer better services

> but also leads them to convey one-way information reflecting the point of view of those countries, and which, above all, allows them to dominate the information market to an extent which borders on cultural aggression...This [is] <u>de facto</u> monopoly. (UNESCO Director General M'Bow, <u>Moving Toward Change</u>, 1976.)

At the New Delhi 1976 Conference of the Non-aligned Press Agencies Pool (NANAP), the major address of NANAP's president Vidya Shukla informed the world that the Western news agencies' monopoly allows:

> only the powerful countries in reality to pump their information into all regions of the world without let or hindrance...perpetuates colonialism, economic exploitation, humiliation, deliberate denial of cultural opportunity.

While it is true that the five major news agencies (including TASS) produce 90 percent of international news, the alleged cultural nationalism of the Western agencies is not at all apparent from the staff structure. AP has eight times as many foreign nationals as reporters and stringers as it has Americans, and full-time AP correspondents who are foreign nationals outnumber Americans by six to one.

UNESCO pumps millions of dollars a year into national and regional news services that are supposed to help break the monopoly of the major wire services. These subsidized news operations are owned and run by governments, which then proceed to establish their own news monopolies in their countries. This is accomplished, in part, by strictly controlling the international news available to their domestic media and filtering the stories carried by the major Western news services. Why such a big fuss about the cultural aggression of news services when the flow of information they provide is strictly regulated by the complaining governments?

A 1977 study found that AP, UPI and Reuters entered about 80 percent of nonaligned countries only through government or government-controlled channels. Private-sector media were allowed to receive only those wire stories passed on by the government gatekeepers.

Could all the wailing about the Western news monopoly simply be a smokescreen to divert attention from the censorship and rigid information control imposed by the complainers? As Elie Abel, Stanford professor and former NBC correspondent, writes, "Those spokesmen who condemn the alleged monopoly of information flowing from the industrial countries all too often represent governments which impose internal monopolies on all incoming and outgoing information...In short, the picture of passive millions in the developing countries awash in a tidal wave of alien information is quite fanciful."

New World Information Order (NWIO)

The New World Information Order (NWIO) is many things to many people. To the West, the proposed NWIO is a scheme that would allow the authoritarian governments of the world to regulate the collection, processing and transmission of news and data across national frontiers...and spell the end of press freedom in the international arena. To the developing countries of the world, the NWIO is a mechanism to reverse the Western domination of news, communications technology and information; and a tool which Third World countries need, if they are to leap into the twentieth century and share in the much-sought-after New World Economic Order, while at the same time maintaining their own distinct cultural identities. To communist-bloc countries the NWIO represents a legitimation of their view that the media are instruments of state policy, and that total control of news and information is a matter of national sovereignty.

The battle over the NWIO began in earnest in 1976. In July, a UNESCO meeting of Latin American countries endorsed the principle of state control over communications for purposes of furthering development. In August, a Nonaligned Movement Summit in Colombia produced a resolution approving a "New Order for Information," calling for governmental control of "national information media." Later that year, at the Nairobi UNESCO Conference, debate raged over the Soviet Draft Declaration on the Mass Media...particularly Article XII, which would have officially approved state control of all foreign and domestic media. The forces were clearly arrayed. The Third World (represented by the Nonaligned Movement), the Soviet/Socialist bloc and UNESCO confronted the nations of the developed world.

UNESCO's official position prior to this time had been directly contrary to the kind of demands made by NWIO supporters, but UNESCO and its Director General Amadou M'Bow quickly picked up the NWIO banner and have since led the charge.

Nowhere is there written down a succinct definition of the proposed NWIO which includes all of its elements. Various aspects of the New World Information Order are discussed throughout this glossary. Its basic outline is as follows: (1) An end to Western domination of the means of international communications (technology); (2) An end to Western domination of the content of international communications in the news and entertainment spheres; (3) Use of both the means and content of communications for the furtherance of national development and retention of national cultural identity.

The proposed method of achieving these aims is to vest absolute power over all media and information, domestic and international, in the hands of government, stripping the private sector of its authority, independence and freedom.

NWIO

(See "New World Information Order.")

Normative Action

This phrase was borrowed from sociologists, but NWIO advocates use it a lot. It sounds like a pleasant kind of thing--as it were, putting things back on an even keel. However, "normative action" is sociological jargon for punishment. The Islamic traditions of public flogging and cutting off thieves' hands fall under the rubric of "normative action." In the UNESCO context, it encompasses such things as expulsion of foreign journalists. And the threat of normative action is used as a kind of bargaining chip. It has been used recently to advance demands for "a right of reply to offset inaccurate or malicious reporting of international news." And the power to take normative action against journalists who write unfavorable stories is an integral part of the NWIO proposal for licensing newspeople (for their protection).

> The publisher of an Arab weekly, Al-Hawadess, wrote an unfavorable article about Syria. Normative action was taken. The writer was kidnapped and murdered by the Syrian regime. (IPI Report, March 1980.)

Objectivity of the Press

The lack of objectivity of the Western press is often criticized, and used as a justification for demanding a New World Information Order. It is claimed that reports in the Western media always show the Third World in a bad light. This alleged bias has been not supported by any compelling facts. (See "Developmental Journalism" above and "Reuters" in the Organizations section.) Most often, complaints by Third World governments about lack of objectivity seem to revolve around stories about governmental corruption.

> A story was carried on the world wire services about police officers in the Indian state of Bihar who put out the eyes of convicts and criminal suspects. The reporter who broke the story was accused of a lack of objectivity. He was called a "subversive and a delinquent." Members of the government accused him of spreading "malicious lies in order to debunk our political system and weaken the morale of our people to fight for freedom and national honor." (C. Irani, of The Statesman, op. cit.)

Those charging lack of objectivity often cite an alleged excessive concentration by the Western media on Third World disaster and crime.

> Only 3 percent of Western media reports about the Third World concern disasters and only 5.7 percent deal with crimes, according to a 1981 study done by the Center for Research in Journalism and Mass Communications at the University of North Carolina.

To be fair, not all of the world's press members are objective in their reporting. But the wire services, who perhaps deserve denunciation least, seem to bear the brunt of accusations of biased, subjective and selective reporting. In fact, the wire services may have done more than anyone to establish objectivity in news reporting. Dr. D. Ranly of the University of Missouri observes that "many believe that objectivity came about not because of some idealistic notion about being fair and objective. The idea of objectivity emerged with the development of the wire service, when reporting had to serve papers on the entire spectrum of the political arena. And because it had to serve everybody, it had to be objective."

Parachute Journalism

Most news organizations are closing down their foreign bureaus, except for a very few in major centers. This means that a reporter and/or a film crew must often fly thousands of miles to cover important stories (assuming that the stories ever come to their attention in the first place). Hence the term "parachute journalism." It costs about $260,000 a year to maintain a correspondent abroad, including salary, communications, rent and other expenses. Because of this expense, most news organizations are cutting back on their foreign bureaus. According to Curtis Prendergast, of Time Inc., this "leads to superficiality and distortion. Nothing can replace the sensitivity to local nuances that a journalist gets from living in a country." This trend is a source of legitimate complaint for developing countries.

In 1945, there were about 2,500 American correspondents posted in foreign countries. By the mid-'70s that number had dwindled to 465. Almost three-fourths of these few intrepid souls who are left are stationed in 10 capitals abroad--London, Paris, Bonn, Rome, Beirut, Tel Aviv, Jerusalem, Tokyo, Hong Kong, and Ottawa. (C. Prendergast; Communications in a Changing World, The Media Institute.)

The Canadian Broadcasting Corporation's African bureau is located in London.

In August 1983 reporters coming out of South Africa were barred from most of the black African nations, including Zimbabwe, Zambia,

Mozambique, Angola, Tanzania and Botswana. The African bureaus of all the major American TV networks and the BBC were headquartered in Johannesburg, South Africa. (The Washington Post, Aug. 3, 1983.)

Pluralism

UNESCO claims that "pluralism" is the opposite of the present one-way information flow from the West to the Third World. In fact, the UNESCO majority likes the concept of a one-way flow. It would simply like to change the direction and control the content. In the name of "pluralism," these countries clamor to see more information about themselves in the Western press. But they want to control exactly what others learn about themselves, because to know your neighbor is not necessarily to love him. And as one commentator noted, "Incessant news regarding instability and difficult political and social conditions can discourage Western investment." Pluralism allegedly describes the ideal world system for information swapping, in which all peoples learn about the others, and gain mutual respect, understanding and confidence. Pluralism is really just one more subterfuge to obscure UNESCO's attempts at legitimizing government control of the international press. Developing countries don't really want their people to learn about the West. In fact, one of the major concerns of Third World governments is that knowledge of the success of Western societies could cause dissatisfaction and rebellion against their own regimes.

Process News

(See the discussions of "Developmental Journalism" and "News," above.) UNESCO's clientele would like to see Western coverage of the Third World's ongoing efforts to cope with problems of development, i.e. the "process." While such stories are not the usual exciting and fast-breaking fare Westerners are used to, this kind of news coverage would be in the spirit of the Helsinki Accords and the UN Constitution. It would increase human understanding and the comity of nations. There is, as usual, a kicker. Process news, by definition, would show developing countries and their governments in a good light. Again, what seems at first blush to be a reasonable type of request or goal, becomes a tool for information control consistent with the entire thrust of the New World Information Order.

Progressive Incorporation of Communications Technology

Whenever you see this phrase, read "nationalization." "Progressive" means progress toward the "democratization" of all media. And democratization often means government control and ownership.

> Broadcast systems exist in 137 countries. But only 28 countries allow private broadcasting. (C.B. Dunham, NBC, Communications in a Changing World; See also, "Information Infrastructure," above.)

Into what is the communications technology being progressively incorporated? Why, national communications policies, of course. New technology acquired by Third World countries is put to the service of government, furthering its policies and enhancing its power. There is no room in this concept for notions of free press and private enterprise. Only governments benefit from this "progressive incorporation." And contrary to the voluble propaganda one hears around UNESCO, government benefit is not, by definition, beneficial to the populations at large.

Propaganda

This is an easy one. According to the West, propaganda is what most of the Second and Third World governments and government-run news services put out. According to those entities, propaganda is what Western governments and news services put out. It all depends whose ox is being gored.

Protection of Journalists

Second and Third World governments argue that journalists need physical protection to carry out their work. The murder and abduction and just plain harassment of journalists in developing countries are cited as evidence of this need. (See "Licensing of Journalists," above.) However, those who "protect" the journalists are in a good position to control what they see and report. What journalists generally need most is protection from governments.

> On August 29, 1983, in Karachi, Pakistan, a mob of several hundred supporters of President Zia attacked eight foreign journalists. Zia's police watched calmly as the reporters were pummeled with fists. Finally, the journalists were placed in protective custody. What fired up the mob in the first place were false reports by the state-controlled (read Zia-controlled) press that named BBC journalist Mark Tully as an instigator of anti-Zia riots in Larkana, Pakistan. One of the foreign correspondents involved, William Claiborne of the Washington Post Foreign Service, suggested that the whole thing was staged by Zia's government to discourage coverage of dissent in Pakistan generally, and reporting of opposition to Zia's declaration of martial law, in

particular. The incident apparently got out of hand when someone threw a bomb into the police compound where the journalists were being held. At least four police were injured in the explosion. (The Washington Post, Aug. 30, 1983.)

Protectionism in International Communications

Economic restraints on the mechanisms of communication provide an effective way for governments to control the content of international communications--one of the major goals of the NWIO.

> Intelsat agreements set payment rates for international information transmissions that are theoretically fair for both transmitters and receivers. However, once the information is inside the receiving country's borders, Intelsat jurisdiction is lost, and many developing countries levy additional local charges on international communications that are higher than the Intelsat costs. Such local charges can, of course, be used as carrots or sticks by the governments involved. (E. Abel, Stanford U., former NBC correspondent and a member of MacBride Commission, op. cit.)

International communications fall outside traditional definitions of goods and services. They are not included in the General Agreement on Tariffs and Trade (GATT) which prohibits dumping, inordinate government excise duties or other support for industries, and many other types of activity detrimental to trading partners.

A recent report by Brazil to the UN Commission on Transnational Corporations describes Brazil's attempt to develop a system that would not only charge for transmission of information, but would tax the information itself, depending on its nature and content.

Implementation of such a scheme will be problematic, but the concept is being actively pursued. The implications for information control are tremendous. And Brazil is very much a role model for other developing countries in the communications field.

Trade protectionism can be used by developing countries to control information and news indirectly, as well. Few countries produce their own newsprint or printing machinery. By establishing a government monopoly over the import of such items, pro-government publications can be rewarded and encouraged, while those critical of the authorities can be disciplined or put out of business.

> Newsprint is more expensive in India than anywhere else in the world. The government controls the importing and allocation of supplies. A 40 percent duty is applied to imports and a further 15 percent <u>ad valorem</u> tax is added. India also imposes a 300 percent duty on the import of printing machinery. Duties may, of course, be waived by the government for individual companies. (C. Irani, op. cit.)

Responsibility of the Press

In many Third World and communist countries, the domestic press is considered a tool of the government. The press is acting "responsibly" only when it works to advance the government's interests and policies. International press agencies and other foreign journalists would be put in the same position under the proposed New World Information Order.

UNESCO's MacBride Commission Report included the following admonition:

Reporting on international events or developments in individual countries in situations of crisis and tension requires extreme care and responsibility.

The MacBride Commission's Recommendation #58 reads in part: "Effective legal measures should be designed to: ...(b) circumscribe the action of transnationals by requiring them to comply with specific criteria and conditions defined by national legislation and development policies." Translation: Governments are invited to pass laws requiring foreign journalists and news services to report what Third World governments tell them to report. Penalties of fines, jail or expulsion would make such legal measures "effective." If the NWIO proposal to license journalists and enforce a Code of Conduct were put into effect, it would be a major step toward this type of journalistic "responsibility." Encouraging press responsibility was one reason given by MacBride himself for urging a licensing scheme.

Right to Communicate

This is a "right" that appears to have been modeled on the First Amendment rights to free speech, but then turned around to suit UNESCO's purpose. According to UNESCO documents this right accrues primarily to countries, not individuals or corporations. It is apparently an attempt to justify the government domination of communications envisioned as part of the NWIO. The right to communicate as it is currently conceived is apparently made up of the following panoply of included rights:

    Right to Inform
    Right to be Informed
    Right to Preservation of Cultural Identity
    Right to Cultural Exchange
    Right to Cultural Integrity
    Right of Opinion and Expression
    Right of Correction (This would be used to force Western media to publish corrections and retractions of alleged errors.)
    Right of Reply (This would justify demands for publication or broadcast of unedited material provided by governments which were offended by news reports, whether or not those reports were true.)

These rights would be available to individuals and corporations only if particular governments wished to allow their exercise. UNESCO documents spell out explicitly that states or "collectives" are superior in interest to individuals. It is also averred that "rights" (which are enjoyed by states) are more fundamental than "freedoms" (which are enjoyed by individuals). Clearly, then, a government exercising its right to communicate may legitimately ignore an individual's or corporation's freedom of expression or freedom of the press.

Role of the Media

In almost all developing countries a major part of the media's role is to advance the social and developmental goals of the country. In practice, these goals include the political goals of the government. Because the media are the vehicles by which news and information reach the people, it follows that the media must be controlled, so that they will report what the government wants reported. Thus, the media's role is to be a tool of the state. This is in direct contrast to one of the most basic aspects of our Western concept of the media's role--to act as an independent watchdog of government, often telling the citizenry precisely what the government does not want reported. In most of the Third World, as in communist countries (where the media are an intrinsic part of the state), criticism of the government by the press is rarely tolerated. Most non-industrialized countries are not shy about expelling foreign journalists who write unflattering truths, sometimes even trivial truths.

> "One Western correspondent was expelled from Zaire because he mentioned that President Mobutu was wearing Israeli paratroop wings." (Mort Rosenblum, while Director of AP's Paris bureau, quoted by Rosemary Righter in *Whose News?*)

Domestic journalists are often subject to discipline tactics to keep them in line--tactics ranging from harassment to murder.

> *Item*: In October 1983 a local Turkish stringer with UPI applied for a passport to go to a UPI training session in London, England. Istanbul police blindfolded, beat and threatened the journalist when he inquired about the progress of his passport application. The application was denied. When UPI pursued the matter, Ankara officials charged the local journalist with a "crime of thought." Under Turkish law, no one with charges hanging over him may be issued a passport. The charges could be mired in the Turkish judicial system for five years, according to the journalist's lawyer. Turkish embassy officials said the charges stemmed from events in 1978 and related to "dissemination of propaganda in violation of republicanism or democratic principles." (*The Washington Post*, Oct. 8, 1983.)

Sovereignty and International Communications

National sovereignty is one of the key items in the arsenal of NWIO advocates. It provides the philosophical and legal justification for every aspect of government control of communications and the press--domestic or international. (See "National Communications Policies," above. Also see "Right to Communicate," above, for discussion of an attempt to develop further legal justifications.) One of the most fundamental concepts in international relations is territorial integrity and the right of a government to sovereignty within its territory. The U.S.S.R. claims that its sovereignty, or absolute authority, extends to all information within, entering or leaving its borders. This is one of the key legal bases for many of the concepts comprising the New World Information Order.

Taxation of Information Flow

(See "Protectionism in International Communications.")

Technology Transfer

(See "Progressive Incorporation of Communications Technology.")

Training of Journalists

Training for Third World journalists is an important part of the NWIO package sought by UNESCO's majority. There is universal agreement in the First, Second and Third Worlds that training is important and necessary. However, there is great disagreement about what training is best. UNESCO funds a number of training programs directly and through the International Program for the Development of Communications (see separate entry in the "Organizations" section). These programs are generally run by governments or government news agencies and stress such things as the media's "proper" role as servants of the state, and reliance on government press releases. Some countries, such as Costa Rica, have established permanent schools for journalists, and require aspiring journalists to graduate before they are allowed to work in the media. Courses addressing similar themes, plus training and education in socialist doctrine, are given by the communist-oriented schools run by the International Organization of Journalists (IOJ, see separate entry). Hundreds of Third World journalists attend. First World news organizations, governments and private organizations provide training courses, seminars and workshops which attempt to increase the journalistic skills of participants and introduce them positively to the Western concept of the Role of the Media (see separate entry).

Representatives of the following countries have attended Western-sponsored programs in the recent past:

> India, Kenya, Thailand, Hong Kong, Venezuela, Colombia, Ecuador, Costa Rica, Panama, Chile, Peru, Brazil, Bangladesh, Ghana, Jamaica, Zambia, Zimbabwe, Philippines, Indonesia, Qatar, Malaysia, Turkey, Dubai, Brunei, Jordan, Kuwait, Sarawak, Kiribali, Tuvalu, Nigeria, Tanzania, Upper Volta, Benin, Syria, Guam, Papua New Guinea, Argentina, Zaire, Libya, Saudi Arabia, Sri Lanka, Liberia. (<u>IPI Report</u>, Jan. 1981.)

(Note: In 1983 a world-wide inventory of training and exchange programs for Third World journalists, called "The List of Talloires," was compiled by George A. Krimsky, AP World News Editor.)

Transnational Corporations

This is a derogatory term in UNESCOese, usually referring to the major Western news agencies such as AP, UPI, Reuters and Agence France-Presse. News wire agencies are generally cooperatives, owned essentially by the clients served. They include Canada's Canadian Press (CP), West Germany's Deutsche Presse-Agentur (DPA), Denmark's Ritzaus Bureau (RB), Finland's Suomen Tietotomisto-Finska Notisbyran (STT-FNB), Italy's Agencia Nationale Stampa Associata (ANSA), Japan's Kyodo and the 13-country Caribbean Commonwealth's Caribbean News Agency (CANA). The transnational news agencies funded by UNESCO do not seem to be included in the UNESCO definition, however. Much of the rhetoric of the NWIO movement is aimed at the Western news agencies. Because AP is the largest Western wire service, it takes a tremendous amount of abuse from advocates of a New World Information Order. AP is described as a greedy, monopolistic, neo-colonialist and cultural imperialist extraordinaire. The company has been roundly criticized because AP stories in Western papers cover only the Third World's tragedies, never its triumphs. This criticism has been refuted by several recent studies. It is also now acknowledged that the Western wire services actually lose money on their Third World coverage. The criticism continues--although perhaps it is becoming less shrill.

Mort Rosenblum, editor of the International Herald Tribune, reported in April 1980 that:

> One UNESCO official, setting up a fact-finding meeting on international news agencies, barred agency representatives. He told one: "You would simply confuse the issues."

Chapter 2: Organizations

2.1 Introduction

The debate raging over the proposed New World Information Order involves many governmental, quasi-governmental, private and international groups. What follows is a list of some of the important players, including a brief note to indicate the nature of the entity and its involvement in international communications issues. A major barrier to understanding New World Information Order (NWIO) issues is the horrendous use of alphabet-soup acronyms. Virtually every organizaton has a hodge-podge of letters to call its own. Descriptions follow only the proper name headings.

2.2 Organizations--Entries

AFP: See, Agence France-Presse.

Agence France-Presse (AFP): A news wire service. (And a Transnational Corporation, in the lingo of the New World Information Order debate.) AFP is one of the big five international news agencies. The other four are AP, UPI, Reuters and TASS (see separate entries). Much of AFP's Third World coverage deals with former French colonies, although AFP operates in more than 140 countries and each day sends out more than three million words of news in four languages. The precursor of AFP was founded in 1835 as the Agence Havas. During World War II, in September 1944, AFP was nationalized. It is now neither fish nor fowl, and can best be described as a *de facto* cooperative, financed both by its subscribing clients and substantial subsidies from the French government. It is governed by an Administrative Council whose members include members of the press and government agencies. AFP still has a sort of flag-waving image relative to its news reports about France, but the agency is generally considered a legitimate, objective news agency.

Agency for International Development (AID): An independent agency of the U.S. government. AID provides money for research and development projects in the Third World. There is a special AID program on the use of telecommunications in development.

AID: See, Agency for International Development.

American Newspaper Publishers Association (ANPA): ANPA was established in 1887. It has a current membership of approximately 1,400 newspapers, including publications in the U.S., Canada, Bermuda, Puerto Rico, Guam, Brazil, Bahamas and the U.S. Virgin Islands. ANPA acts as a clearinghouse for information about virtually every aspect of the newspaper business, and publishes many reports. ANPA's headquarters is in Reston, Virginia. ANPA members oppose the New World Information Order.

American Society of Newspaper Editors (ASNE): ASNE was founded in 1922. Its current membership of 900 includes working editors from U.S. and Canadian daily newspapers. ASNE's headquarters is in Reston, Virginia, where it publishes The Bulletin nine times a year. ASNE's formal position on UNESCO's activities is that ASNE monitors the ongoing debate and "in cooperation with other news organizations actively opposes any proposal that threatens press freedom."

ANPA: See, American Newspaper Publishers Association.

AP: See, Associated Press.

Arab Revolutionary News Agency (ARNA): A nice example of where UNESCO money goes, this Arab-African news agency was established in 1977 (with UNESCO assistance) in line with UNESCO's drive to establish alternatives to the major Western news agencies. Also in line with UNESCO's philosophy, the ARNA is under strict government control. And the principal mover and shaker in ARNA's formation was President Muammar Khadafy of Libya. ARNA serves most black African and Arab countries in Africa and the Middle East. ARNA's stated goals include fostering the "liberation" of African and Arab countries. The news agency has been called a "politically driven propaganda machine" by Western observers. A revolutionary colleague of Khadafy calls it an instrument for the "liberation of thought."

ARNA: See, Arab Revolutionary News Agency.

ASNE: See, American Society of Newspaper Editors.

Associated Press (AP): Another of the major Western news services referred to as Transnational Corporations (see separate entries for Agence France-Presse, UPI and Reuters). AP was founded in 1848 by six New York newspapers and is now a non-profit cooperative corporation with about 4,800 "members" and a board of directors. AP's media members are responsible for financing the system should it operate at a loss. Non-member "subscribers" pay a fee for access to AP "wire" reports. AP's staff of about 2,500 send out almost two million words a day to more than 15,000 media outlets--3,700 radio and TV stations in the U.S., 1,400 U.S. newspapers and more than 10,000 media outlets in approximately 110 countries. The reports are sent over more than 800,000 miles of leased wire in the U.S., and ocean cables, land-lines and radiowaves to overseas subscribers. AP, because of its size and importance, is the most frequent target of proponents of the NWIO. They condemn Western news services as monopolistic agents of economic and cultural imperialism. (See glossary entry, "News Monopoly.")

Center for Strategic and International Studies (CSIS): A "think tank" organization affiliated with Georgetown University, Washington D.C. Since 1975, CSIS has published several books condemning the NWIO, warning of the impending showdown between the haves and have-nots in international communications, and graphically describing the extremely high stakes involved.

Communications Satellite Corporation (COMSAT): COMSAT was established by federal legislation in 1962. It is a private corporation, designated as the official U.S. representative to INTELSAT. (See separate entry, "International Satellite Organization.") COMSAT's 15-member board of directors includes three members appointed by the President and confirmed by the Senate.

COMSAT: See, Communications Satellite Corporation.

CSIS: See, Center for Strategic and International Studies.

ECOSOC: See, United Nations Economic and Social Council.

FCC: See, Federal Communications Commission.

Federal Communications Commission (FCC): In addition to its domestic regulation duties, the FCC joins members of other government departments and agencies (such as the Department of State and the United States Information Agency) as U.S. representatives at international conferences in a number of technical areas, such as frequency allocations, international common carrier matters, and broadcast standards. The FCC's Office of Science and Technology; Common Carrier Bureau; Mass Media Bureau; and the International Telecommunications Advisor are involved in these activities. The FCC also works with the International Telecommunications Union (see separate entry) to coordinate the American aspects of a telecommunications training program. (See separate glossary entry, "Training of Journalists.") This training program is funded by the United Nations Development Program (see separate entry).

Freedom House: The goal of this 4,000-member organization, founded in 1941, is to strengthen free institutions at home and abroad. It now has a staff of about 18 people at its New York headquarters. Its executive director, Leonard Sussman, is an outspoken American leader in the fight against the NWIO. In 1967 Freedom House established the Freedom House Public Affairs Institute as a research publication center. The annual publication Freedom in the World documents the levels of freedom, including press freedom, in all countries of the world.

IAPA: See, Inter American Press Association.

IBI: See, Intergovernmental Bureau of Informatics.

IFRB: See, International Frequency Registration Board.

INEX: A privately financed news agency cooperative headquarterd in Manila. INEX covers the First and Second Worlds for the benefit of media in the Third World. INEX attempts to provide a legitimate news service without political or ideological bias.

INTELSAT: See, International Telecommunications Satellite Organization.

Inter American Press Association (IAPA): This association of more than 1,000 publications from 31 Western Hemisphere countries was established in 1942. IAPA works to improve the protection of freedom of the press and peoples' right to know in North and South America. IAPA is strongly against the governmental control of media which is advocated by NWIO supporters.

Intergovernmental Bureau of Informatics (IBI): A spin-off from UNESCO, now headquartered in Rome as an independent organization. IBI has 35 members, mostly Third World countries. IBI promotes international data-processing policies that would "lessen dependence on Western companies." IBI is currently studying the relationship of transborder data flow and sovereignty. IBI funding comes principally from France.

International Commission for the Study of Communications Problems (MacBride Commission--UNESCO):
UNESCO's 1977-79 Commission was chaired by Irish jurist Sean MacBride. The final report was released in 1980, and is one of the most important documents to come out of UNESCO, although it does not represent official UNESCO policy. But with its 85 background papers, it gives great insight into UNESCO's concerns and the direction UNESCO is likely to take in the future. The Report praised the Western notion of access to information, and it condemned censorship. But these positive aspects were undercut by recommendations advocating subservience of news media to governmental "social, cultural, economic and political goals." Other recommendations displayed a strong bias against private ownership of news media and the (undocumented) "problems created in a society by advertising." MacBride himself wrote a paper discussing the licensing/protection of journalists in a favorable light. The MacBride Commission provided a wonderful soapbox for promoters of the New World Information Order and critics of the Western news media. Mort Rosenblum, editor of the International Herald Tribune, described the Report in relatively mild terms. He called it "deceptive and double-edged...the objection [in the Report] was not simply to inadequate reporting; it was to accurate reporting of embarrassing information...In one UNESCO working document, I found my own writings quoted five times, always out of context...."

International Frequency Registration Board (IFRB):
The part of the International Telecommunications Union that records and administers spectrum use by various countries.

International Organization of Journalists (IOJ):
The IOJ is an organization of communist/socialist journalists, claiming 150,000 members in 109 countries. Founded in 1946, its headquarters is

in Prague. The IOJ strongly supports the NWIO and government control of all media and communications in the Third World. It works hand-in-glove with UNESCO on Third World communications issues, including programs for the "education of democratic, anti-imperialist and anti-colonialist journalists." Hundreds of Third World newspeople have graduated from the IOJ's two training centers in East Berlin and Budapest. The former President of the IOJ, Finland's Kaarle Nordenstreng, is on Finland's National Commission for UNESCO; he has been influential in establishing UNESCO policy for the last decade, and he helped draft the Russian Draft Declaration on use of the media that would have legitimized the principle of government control of the press.

International Press Institute (IPI): IPI is a London-based organization to defend freedom of the press and protect journalists from harassment, persecution and suppression. IPI was founded in 1951 and currently has abut 1,800 individual members, including broadcast and print news editors, news directors, staff members who deal with news policy, educators and foreign correspondents. IPI conducts research on news sources, foreign news reporting and the flow of news. Occasional studies of problems in international journalism are published by IPI, in addition to its regular monthly publication, IPI Report.

International Program for the Development of Communication (IPDC): A UNESCO spinoff that was orginally to (a) provide a clearing house for communications development needs, resources and priorities, and (b) exchange information and arrange consultations so that developed and developing countries might cooperate more effectively. IPDC has become a funds-dispensing entity, giving millions of dollars to developing countries for their own government-controlled news agencies ($3 million in 1982). Only eight of the 35 IPDC members are Western countries. The Cuban delegate stated flatly in 1981 that the IPDC is "a tool for change on a political basis." The U.S. does not contribute funds to IPDC, preferring to give assistance in this area bilaterally, i.e. directly to particular Third World countries and programs.

International Telecommunications Satellite Organization (INTELSAT): INTELSAT maintains a satellite system for global commercial telecommunications on behalf of its members (108 countries and associated operating entities). It was founded in 1964, with its headquarters in Washington, D.C. INTELSAT maintains six satellites in operation, with 10 spares in orbit. (Each satellite has an operating life expectancy of only seven years.) INTELSAT carries two-thirds of all transoceanic international communications. The organization sets fee structures for use of the system by member governments and other private entities. Of late, the NWIO debate has included INTELSAT functions and infused an element of politicization into what was originally designed to be a strictly technical regulatory body. For example, developing countries are demanding that they be allocated frequency slots and satellite orbital positions, even though their governments have neither the satellites, nor the funds, to utilize such allocations.

International Telecommunications Union (ITU): ITU is the umbrella organization administering the various international agreements on international broadcasting and communications services fees and technical standards, including WARC, RARC, and IFRB matters (see other entries). ITU has 157 member nations and is headquartered in Geneva. The activities of the ITU have become increasingly politicized in recent years. For example, at its June/July 1983 Regional Administrative Radio Conference meetings, Argentina used the forum to further its claims to the Falklands/Malvinas

Islands. The ITU manages projects of the United Nations Development Program, providing aid to developing countries in the telecommunications area, including technical assistance and personnel training programs. Thus, ITU is under increasing pressure to expand aid to the Third World and advance the NWIO agenda.

Inter Press Service (IPS): A unique organization in many respects, it was established in 1964 with the stated goal of fostering "understanding of the cultural, political, social and economic realities of the Third World." IPS focuses primarily on Latin America, sending news and features to other areas of the Third World. IPS is headquartered in Buenos Aires and Rome and is owned by individual journalists, not newspapers or broadcasting corporations. IPS operates free of any socialist or political bias and any profits are re-invested to expand the service.

IOJ: See, International Organization of Journalists.

IPDC: See, International Program for the Development of Communication.

IPI: See, International Press Institute.

IPS: See, Inter Press Service.

ITU: See, International Telecommunications Union.

MacBride Commission: See, International Commission for the Study of Communications Problems.

NANAP: See, Nonaligned Press Agencies Pool.

News Agency Cooperatives: These are international news agencies owned by the principal broadcast and print media clients served. Most will allow subscribers access to their reports for a fee.

Most major wire services are client-owned (the major exceptions are United Press International and, as of August 1984, Reuters), including Associated Press, Agence France-Presse (AFP), Canada's Canadian Press (CP), Denmark's Ritzaus Bureau (RB), Finland's Suomen Tietotomisto-Finska Notisbyran (STT-FNB), Italy's Agencia Nationale Stampa Associata (ANSA), Japan's Kyodo and the 13-country Caribbean Commonwealth's Caribbean News Agency (CANA). By way of contrast, virtually all the Third World national and regional news agencies (approximately 120) are owned by governments. According to Freedom in the World 1983-1984, 95 percent of the countries with the lowest civil liberties rating have government-owned national news agencies.

National Telecommunication and Information Administration (NTIA): NTIA is part of the Department of Commerce. NTIA's principal responsibilities are to develop and formulate U.S. policy regarding technical standards for international communications, regulation of transborder flows, and privacy protection in international information trade. NTIA personnel participate in training programs, which are organized by other government and private-sector agencies for the benefit of Third World communications specialists. NTIA officials also attend international conferences as part of U.S. delegations.

Nonaligned Press Agencies Pool (NANAP): NANAP was established at the July 1976 Conference of Nonaligned Nations. Its headquarters is in Prague, Czechoslovakia. The government-run Yugoslavian national news agency TANJUG (Telegrafska Agencija Nova Jugoslavia) organized the pool. NANAP members (national news agencies run by the governments of developing countries) provide propagandistic "news" releases to NANAP, which, in turn passes them along unedited to other national news agencies. NANAP was set up by the Group of 77, as the nonaligned countries were then known, as an alternative to reliance on Western news services. NANAP's aim is to allow developing countries to "exchange and circulate information on...mutual achievements," and provide "authentic information" about their countries to the press of other developing nations. (See also the glossary entry "Correct and Factual Information" for greater appreciation of how NANAP operates.) The same 1976 conference that established NANAP saw the first formal use of the phrase, "New International Order in Matters of Information," soon to become known as the NWIO, and NANAP was intended as the first step toward its achievement.

NTIA: See, National Telecommunication and Information Administration.

OECD: See, Organization for Economic Co-operation and Development.

Organization for Economic Co-operation and Development (OECD): The Paris-based OECD comprises 24 members from the world's industrialized Western nations. OECD analyzes policy and provides a forum for negotiating voluntary agreements among its members. Five of OECD's standing committees deal with international communications issues, including transborder data flow and personal privacy concerns. The OECD is concerned primarily with the economic implications in these areas and has taken no formal position on the essentially political demands for a New World Information Order.

RARC: See, Regional Administrative Radio Conference.

Regional Administrative Radio Conference (RARC): The various RARCs are parts of the International Telecommunications Union organization. The U.S. belongs to Region 2, which covers North and South

America. There are two other RARCs. Region 1 includes Europe, Africa and North Asia. Region 3 includes the bulk of Asia and the South Pacific. Negotiations and agreements over technical standards affecting neighbors are dealt with in these geographically restricted meetings. More-universal issues are debated in the World Administrative Radio Conference (WARC). Recent RARC meetings have seen conflict between the U.S. and its less affluent neighbors. Brazil, for example, objected to standards proposed by the U.S. for minimum strength signals for Direct Broadcast Satellites. Brazil has tremendous rainfall so it wouldn't benefit from the higher power signals, and Brazil was also concerned about "signal invasion" across its borders. A majority of Third World countries at the conference voted against the U.S. on the issue.

Reuters: Reuters is based in London, England. It is one of the world's five major press agencies, and was founded in 1851. Until 1984 it was a limited company, owned by four associations representing the British national newspapers (Newspaper Publishers Association), United Kingdom regional papers including Ireland (Press Association), Australian papers (Australia Associated Press), and New Zealand papers (New Zealand Press Association). Reuters, which has recently authorized public trading of its stock, has perhaps the greatest array of services. It operates in more than 150 countries and produces news reports in six languages. But in terms of volume of news moved per day, Reuters is outdone by both Agence France-Presse and AP. In a 1976 interview with Rosemary Righter (author of Whose News?), Gerry Long, managing director of Reuters, refuted Third World charges that Western news dominates the wire services. Long pointed out that in Reuters services to Africa, 65-70 percent was news about other African countries, Third World activities at the United Nations and news of other developing countries in the world.

TASS: TASS was created in 1925. It is now the official federal information agency for the Union of Soviet Socialist Republics, and is responsible to the Council of Ministers. The news agencies of the other Republics are subordinate to TASS, (e.g. RATAU of the Ukraine, BELTA of Byelorusia, UZTAG of Uzbekistan) and act as TASS correspondents. TASS has more than 325 foreign subscribers. Like all communist news agencies, TASS maintains as one of its basic tenets that all reporting must serve the interests of the state. Part of its formal charter describes its function as disseminating "information about the achievements of real socialism in economy, science and culture, publicize the Soviet way of life, expose the concoctions and slander of bourgeois ideology." In socialist countries, press agencies are usually part of the government itself, and have a monopoly on providing news in the country, e.g. East Germany's Allgemeiner Deutscher Nachrictendienst (ADN). One of the "operating principles" of TASS is that its information be based on fact. It is interesting to note that one of the few other news agencies to specifically include this as a basic principle in its charter is the privately owned, for-profit UPI.

UN: See, United Nations.

UNCITRAL: See, United Nations Commission on International Trade Law.

UNCTAD: See, United Nations Conference on Trade and Development.

UNCTC: See, United Nations Commission on Transnational Corporations.

UNDP: See, United Nations Development Program.

UNESCO: See, United Nations Educational, Scientific and Cultural Organization.

United Nations (UN): The United Nations organization proper deals only infrequently with international communications. However, a number of the UN's specialized bodies have continuing responsibility in this area, not just UNESCO. Such bodies are listed under their own names. It may appear that some of the agencies listed below are doing much the same things as others. The UN and its agencies are heavily bureaucratized and duplication of effort is sometimes the result.

United Nations Commission on International Trade Law (UNCITRAL): UNCITRAL's aim is to standardize international trade law as much as possible. The pronouncements of a body such as UNCITRAL could be very useful in focusing and sorting out the freewheeling debate over NWIO matters. If areas of agreement and disagreement in international communications law were established, developed and developing countries could engage in a dialogue with some common basis of understanding. UNCITRAL is looking at international trade law relating to telecommunications, but there is precious little to look at. The field is so new that frequently there has been no custom or usage established--and therefore, nothing to form the basis of international law. As a result, UNCITRAL has, to date, been unable to provide much leadership in NWIO issues.

United Nations Commission on Transnational Corporations (UNCTC): One of the UNCTC's principal goals is to give Third World countries some combined clout in negotiating with transnational corporations, including corporations like AP which are involved in international communications. The majority of UNCTC members are governments of developing countries, and UNCTC spends a great deal of time and money conducting research which individual Third World countries could not afford on their own. UNTC then provides coaching, education and information to governments of developing countries negotiating with transnationals. Part of UNTC's energies have been directed at forcing transnationals to comply with a Code of Ethics drafted at the Commission. (See separate entry "Code of Ethics" for UNESCO's activities in this area as part of the NWIO.)

United Nations Conference on Trade and Development (UNCTAD): UNCTAD is one of the largest UN bodies, with a membership of 166 that includes countries and other UN special bodies. UNCTAD is specifically mandated to promote trade (including telecommunications) between countries at differing stages of economic development. UNCTAD funds research and study projects on trade issues and sponsors conferences designed to bring various countries together and generate further international trade agreements. For funding of industrial development projects or communications improvements that would enable developing countries to take advantage of the trade agreements identified and encouraged by UNCTAD, governments look to other agencies such as UNDP (United Nations Development Program--see separate entry), whose principal function is to dispense funds. UNCTAD works very closely with ECOSOC (United Nations Economic and Social Council--see separate entry).

United Nations Development Progam (UNDP): One of the newer organizations, UNDP operates major UN programs and funds more than 5,000 projects, including projects for technical cooperation in the transfer of communications technology between developed and developing countries. UNDP was created in 1965 to act as a central source of grant funding and coordination for the entire UN system. While UNDP's staff of more than 5,800 people dispenses almost a billion dollars a year, other agencies (e.g. UNESCO) still fund projects on their own.

United Nations Economic and Social Council (ECOSOC): This group encourages a general sharing of the wealth among nations, through cooperation in educational, cultural and economic matters. ECOSOC is mainly a deliberative body, unlike UNESCO which pays for and carries out substantive projects. The UNCTC (United Nations Commission on Transnational Corporations--see separate entry) is a subsidiary of ECOSOC.

United Nations Educational, Scientific, and Cultural Organization (UNESCO): UNESCO was one of the first specialized agencies of the United Nations formed after World War II. UNESCO has 166 members, including virtually every country in the world, as well as other organizations and UN agencies. The UNESCO budget is currently in the range of $200 million per year, of which the U.S. contributes 25 percent. UNESCO, through its staff of almost 4,000, carries out a plenitude of projects ranging from providing assistance to developing countries in preserving cultural artifacts and oral histories, to literacy programs and conferences designed to help Third World countries acquire scientific technology and expertise from developed countries. Of most concern here is UNESCO's apparent leadership in the drive to impose a New World Information Order (NWIO) on the world. Much of this activity in the heavily bureaucratized UNESCO takes place in the Division of Development of Communications Systems and Division of Free Flow of Information. UNESCO's first serious interest in the formulation of mass communications policies started in the late 1960s. At that point, UNESCO worked toward the goal of a free flow of information among nations, unimpeded by any country's domestic laws and policies. Recently, however, UNESCO has done an about-face and now battles, in the name of the NWIO, to overthrow the free flow doctrine. During the period 1972-1978, debate raged over the Soviet-inspired Draft Declaration on Uses of the Mass Media, which most Western countries saw as a thinly disguised attempt to legitimize state control over news and international communications. Several countries, including the U.S., walked out of UNESCO temporarily over the issue. In 1976 UNESCO, and its Director General Amadou M'Bow began to espouse the cause of a NWIO. To Westerners, the proposed New Order is worse than the previous attempt to simply legitimate government control over news and information. It is a mechanism for encouraging and funding its actual occurrence. The U.S. is now considering leaving UNESCO permanently, partly in concern over the NWIO issue.

United Press International (UPI): UPI was, until recently, the largest commercial news agency run for profit (a public offering of Reuters' stock usurped UPI's lead in 1984). Based in the United States, UPI is registered as a limited private corporation and is a regular commercial enterprise. The company was formed in 1958 when the United Press merged with the International News Service. Much of UPI's foreign news service involves Latin America, but the company has subscribers in more than 110 countries around the world. There are some other private, for-profit news agencies in the world, notably in Mexico and Portugal, but they restrict themselves primarily to national news. UPI is the only "world-class" commercial news service.

United States Department of State: The State Department is the site of principal responsibility for American foreign affairs. In the international information and telecommunications areas the State Department coordinates the participation of U.S. officials in major international conferences and organizatons, in addition to coordinating U.S. government efforts in substantive policy-making. The Undersecretary for Security Assistance, Science and Technology is the chairperson of the Senior Interagency Group for International Communication and Information Policy. The Director of the Office of Communications and UNESCO affairs in the Bureau of International Organizations Affairs analyzes and recommends policy regarding the NWIO and free flow of information debate in all UN agencies.

United States National Commission for UNESCO: The Commission was established in 1946 by an act of Congress. Its role is to act as a liaison agency among UNESCO, the U.S. government and the American people. The Commission has 100 members--60 representatives of national voluntary organizations; 25 local, state and federal officials; and 15 citizens appointed by the Secretary of State for outstanding contributions in the fields of education, science and culture. The Commission, based in Washington, D.C., is responsible to the Secretary of State, and produces public information about UNESCO and its activities.

United States Information Agency (USIA): The USIA is the major U.S. government agency dealing with international information, cultural and educational exchange. It has varied responsibilities in the area of telecommunications and information policy, including Voice of America activities and funding programs for the education of Third World journalists. Such projects include the well-known Fulbright Program and the International Visitors Program. The USIA also provides funds to private-sector organizations for research and publications on international communications issues.

United States Trade Representative (USTR): This Cabinet-level office plays a major role in coordinating U.S. policy on international trade matters, including telecommunications hardware, technology, and information processing services.

Universal Postal Union (UPU): The UPU is a specialized UN agency with 166 member countries. The precursor to the UPU was established in 1874 to ensure cooperation among postal services and the delivery of international mail. This is still UPU's function. UPU has a tiger by the tail regarding electronic mail systems. The confusion of telecommunications and regular mail systems confuses the UPU deliberations on tariff rates and subsidization of mail services, and political issues are cropping up at UPU, similar to those impeding the ITU's work (International Telecommunications Union--see separate entry).

UPI: See, United Press International.

UPU: See, Universal Postal Union.

USIA: See, United States Information Agency.

USTR: See, United States Trade Representative.

WARC: See, World Administrative Radio Conference discussed at Regional Administrative Radio Conference entry, above.

World Press Freedom Committee: This group of 32 journalistic organizatons was activated in 1976. Its members include editors, publishers and broadcasters from the free-world media, in addition to associations of Dutch and American journalists. Among its affiliates are organizations from Spain, Canada, Venezuela, Colombia, Argentina, Australia and the Caribbean. It has been an activist force in the area of Third World communications issues, fighting "those who advocate state-controlled media; those who seek to deny truth in news; and those who abuse newsmen." From its Washington, D.C. headquarters, WPFC gives direct aid to the press in developing countries through more than 75 projects in Asia, Africa, Latin America and the Caribbean. WPFC assistance includes money, training programs, technical advice, equipment and conference participation.

WPFC: See, World Press Freedom Committee.

Appendix A: Government Actions And Press Freedom 1981-82

The following compilation illustrates the problems faced by journalists throughout the world. It is in no way exhaustive. Amnesty International documented approximately 300 cases of intimidation of journalists in 1982 alone, including torture, imprisonment, kidnapping and murder. The reporting here of more or fewer incidents is not intended to reflect on the state of press freedom in any particular country. But notice that there are few "incidents" in those countries where the government has already swallowed up the media completely, along with other private institutions--namely, communist countries.

The list of incidents worldwide (during the last half of 1981 and 1982) involved press freedom, or lack thereof. It was drawn from a number of sources, but substantial reliance was placed on reports published by the International Press Institute (IPI)--a European-based organization, with American representatives, whose goal is to defend freedom of the press and protect journalists from harassment, persecution and suppression.

1981:

June--Guyana--The Catholic Standard (a publication of the Roman Catholic church and critical of the government) suspended publication because of a lack of newsprint. At the same time the government-owned paper, the Chronicle, started a new Sunday supplement which was bigger than the entire Catholic Standard. The Guyanese government controls newsprint allocation.

July--Sri Lanka--The government announced a new requirement for newspapers to post financial security against possible defamation actions, putting serious pressure on the small minority of papers that are not government owned. The Cabinet decides on a case-by-case basis how much money is needed for security.

September--Pakistan--A publisher, Irshad Rao, was sentenced to 12 months in jail and his paper was banned for publishing anti-state material. After his sentence was completed, the government held Rao three more months for "security reasons."

September--Suriname--General press censorship was introduced to "protect the population against unjust and malicious reporting," according to the Suriname News Agency.

October--India--Prime Minister Indira Gandhi admitted censoring mail of journalists, among others. She criticized the foreign media as working according to the dictum, "Bad news is good news and good news is no news."

December--Indonesia--The Jakarta daily Sinar Harapan reported that in 1981, 49 events had been subjects of a government ban on coverage, including visits to parliament of delegations submitting complaints.

1982:

January--Ghana--Following the December 1981 coup, the editors of two of Ghana's national newspapers were fired by Flt. Lt. Jerry Rawlings' Provisional National Defense Council to "rid the country of all kinds of corruption." Later in October, all papers were banned except those granted a government license.

January--Guatemala--The editor of the anti-government paper La Nacion was machine-gunned to death near his home.

January--Poland--After martial law was declared, 400 Solidarity papers, with a cumulative circulation of 1.5 million, were shut down. (Possession of underground papers is punishable by three to five years in prison.) More than 150 journalists were interned in camps. After "ideological screening" about 1,200 newsmen were fired and 1,200 were demoted. The independent Association of Polish Journalists (SDP) was disbanded and replaced by a government-controlled body.

January--Thailand--The Asian Wall Street Journal was banned from sale and distribution indefinitely after publishing an article questioning the future existence of the Thai monarchy.

February--Turkey--All quotations from foreign radio and press were banned by the government. And all copies of the magazine Hyat (Life) were seized for breach of Decree 52 that prohibits all public discussion of politics. The magazine contained an article written by former Prime Minister Suleyman Demiral.

March--Turkey--The country's leading female columnist, Nazli Ilcak, was sentenced to nine months in jail for violating Decree 52. She referred to the ongoing trial of 220 Action Party officials charged with plotting a coup.

March--Uganda--The last foreign journalist was expelled and the government announced that only "qualified, objective, bona fide journalists" would be accepted by Uganda in the future.

April--India--Two papers in Bihar province were forced to close by government-backed unions after the papers reported on government corruption and police atrocities. Mrs. Gandhi urged the domestic press to concentrate on Development Journalism and not "political minutiae."

April--Indonesia--The leading weekly Tempo was suspended from publication because it printed a story about the election campaign that "conflicted with official accounts." The magazine reported on a riot at a political rally in which three people were killed, 60 injured and 300 arrested.

April--Malaysia--At the beginning of the election campaign Sheik Osman, The New Strait Times' top political reporter, was forced to take a vacation while the ruling political party (which controlled the paper) was given lopsided and biased coverage during the campaign.

May--Argentina--During the Falklands/Malvinas war, several papers were closed down; editors of the rest were told they would be jailed if they reported any news to "damage the morale of the population"; and Norwegian, French and Swedish journalists were expelled.

June--Nicaragua--A government-backed squad kidnapped and severely beat the editor of La Prensa, one of the country's most influential papers.

July--Thailand--Journalist Barry Wain was thrown out of the country, after working there for three years, for writing an article describing the Vietnamese refugee camps as more like prisons than camps.

August--Afghanistan--After barring journalists

from the country, the government banned the import, ownership and use of film and recording equipment. The Ministry of Information and Culture said the ban was to protect the "morality, religion and traditions of the nation."

August--Kenya--The government suppressed news of an abortive coup attempt by banning the British publications <u>New Africa</u> and <u>Africa Now</u>, and cutting a two-page article out of <u>Time</u> magazine before allowing it to be distributed.

September--Argentina--The domestic press was officially ordered not to cover certain issues, principally "los desaparecidos" (the thousands of people, many of them journalists, who have disappeared since the mid-1970s).

September--Brazil--Three journalists of the left-wing <u>Hors de Poyo</u> were given prison sentences of three years and three months for printing allegations that some government officials maintained Swiss bank accounts.

September--Indonesia--The Publishers Business License Law went into effect. To effect one of its expressed goals, "less freedom and more responsibility for the press," government representatives were placed on the previously independent Press Council to enforce greatly increased penalties for violations of the press law.

September--Iran--The government reported executing 30 journalists, imprisoning 200 more and firing without compensation the last remaining professional working journalists in the country. Twenty newsmen were also declared "missing." By December 1982, circulation of the largest daily, <u>Kayhan</u>, was down to 15,000 from almost one million in 1978.

September--Malta--The opposition National Party

was broadcasting into Malta from Sicily because it was banned from domestic radio and TV. The ban on National Party programming was extended to include all foreign broadcasts. Local publishing of foreign TV and radio schedules was declared an offense as well.

October--Argentina--Le Semana was closed down by the government for lampooning a state TV scriptwriter, and indirectly the army, thereby committing "degrading actions against essential institutions in the country." The Falklands/Malvinas war had been over for months.

October--Bangladesh--The press was declared subject to official "guidance and advice." The government already required the members of the press to rent their office space and printing presses from the state, and controlled access to newsprint via import licenses.

October--Bulgaria--Kiril Yanev, deputy editor of the daily Otechestven Front reported that government officials physically edit newspaper stories prior to publication.

October--Chile--Of the 3,000 Chilean nationals working as journalists, 400 were killed, imprisoned or banned from writing, and 400 more were forced to leave the country.

October--India--All TV broadcasting, including news, became the responsibility of a government department, to be run by civil servants.

November--Turkey--The editor/columnist of the left-wing daily Cumhuriyet was arrested and charged with the crime of commenting on the new constitution before its adoption.

December--Malaysia--The government declared that it would implement a system suggested at a UNESCO meeting, in which no media would be allowed to receive AP or UPI wire stories directly. Instead a government press agency would distribute the incoming information.

December--Mexico--The government forced closure of one privately owned news service and crippled two antagonistic newspapers by cutting off government advertisements. Up to 50 percent of the ads in Mexican papers and magazines are paid for by the government.

December--Zambia--The government introduced legislation setting up a Code of Conduct for journalists and a 13-member Press Council to enforce the code and punish violations. The press would be allowed only four members on the Press Council.

Appendix B: Selected Bibliography And Suggested Readings

What follows is a brief list of books, collections of essays/speeches, periodicals and UNESCO documents. In the author's opinion they provide valuable insights into the issues raised by the proposed New World Information Order. This list represents only a tiny fraction of the available material. Inclusion of a certain document or exclusion of another is not meant to be construed as a comment of the quality, or lack thereof, of that particular document.

Books and Monographs

Gastil, Raymond D., Freedom in the World--Political Rights and Civil Liberties 1983-1984, 474 pp., Freedom House, Inc., New York, 1984.

Kelly, Sean, Access Denied--The Politics of Press Censorship, 80 pp., "The Washington Papers," Vol. VI, No. 55; Sage Publications, Beverly Hills and London, 1978.

Resource Book for International Communications, 62 pp., The Media Institute, Washington, D.C., 1983.

Righter, Rosemary, Whose News? The Press and

the Third World, 272 pp., The New York Times Book Co., Inc., New York, 1978.

Starrels, John, The U.S.--Third World Conflict: A Glossary, 70 pp., The Heritage Foundation, Washington, D.C., 1983.

Sussman, Leonard R., Mass News Media and the Third World Challenge, 80 pp., "The Washington Papers," Vol. V, No. 46; Sage Publications, Beverly Hills and London, 1977.

Sussman, Leonard R., Warning of a Bloodless Dialect: Glossary for International Communications, 107 pp., The Media Institute, Washington, D.C., 1983.

Yurow, Jane, Issues in International Telecommunications Policy: A Sourcebook, 379 pp., Federal Communications Bar Association and the International Law Institute of Georgetown University, Washington, D.C., 1983.

Collections of Essays/Remarks

Communications in a Changing World, Vols. I-IV, The Media Institute, Washington, D.C., 1983.

Future of the Free Press, (Proceedings of the First World Media Conference, New York, 1978) New World Communications, Inc., New York, 1979.

The Media Crisis, World Press Freedom Committee, Miami, 1980.

The Media Crisis...A Continuing Challenge, World Press Freedom Committee, Washington, D.C., 1982.

Periodicals

> Index on Censorship
>
> IPI Report (Monthly publication of International Press Institute, London)
>
> UNESCO Courier (Monthly publication of UNESCO)
>
> World Press Freedom Review (Annual publication of International Press Institute)
>
> World Press Review

UNESCO Documents

> UNESCO Medium-Term Plan 1983-1988
>
> For the Free Flow of Ideas, 24 pp., UNESCO, 1978.
>
> Many Voices, One World, 312 pp., (Report of the International Commission for the Study of Communication Problems) UNESCO, 1980.

Appendix C: U.S. Government—International Communications Policy

At the time of writing, the locus of decision-making on international communications issues is a matter of vigorous debate within the federal government. Thus, the exact nature of responsibility held by the following offices and individuals is unclear. What follows is not an exhaustive list of those with responsibility in the area of international communications. But it should also be obvious, given the diversity and length of this incomplete list of policymakers, that rationalization of the existing system is necessary and overdue. Many U.S. problems in the international communications arena can be traced to a lack of coordinated and coherent policies.

Office of the President

The chief executive is ultimately responsible for the conduct of America's foreign affairs, including information and communications issues. The following come under the direct control of the President in their areas of concern—national security, foreign intelligence, and foreign trade.

1. National Security Council

2. National Foreign Assessment Center

3. Central Intelligence Agency

4. United States Trade Representative (See glossary entry.)

State Department

State is the site of principal responsibility for American foreign affairs. The Department coordinates the participation of U.S. officials in major international conferences and organizatons, in addition to coordinating international communications and information policymaking in general.

1. Interagency Task Force: The Undersecretary for Security Assistance, Science & Technology is Chairman of the Senior Interagency Group for International Communication and Information Policy.

2. Legal Advisors Office: This office deals with analysis of the legal aspects of ITU, transborder data flow, telecommunications trade policy and international trade operations.

3. Bureau of Economic and Business Affairs: The Director of the Office of International Communications Policy participates with other agencies in formulating policy in the area of ITU negotiating positions, transborder data flow and international regulation of communications in general; and provides participants for international conferences on these matters.

4. Bureau of International Organizations Affairs: The Director of the Office of Communications and UNESCO Affairs analyzes and recommends policy regarding the New

World Information Order and free flow of information debate in all the UN agencies.

5. Bureau of Oceans and International Environmental & Scientific Affairs: The bureau provides coordination for policy matters involving telecommunications technology and other matters involving international communications.

Department of Commerce

The National Telecommunications and Information Administration deals with the FCC in INTELSAT matters. (See glossary entry.)

Department of Defense

DOD is intensely concerned about spectrum allocation in the international sphere, because of the vast portions of spectrum utilized by DOD in its operations domestically and throughout the world.

Federal Communications Commission

(See glossary entry.)

Agency for International Development

(See glossary entry.)

United States Information Agency

USIA is the agency with the major responsibility for U.S. international cultural and information exchange. (See glossary entry.)

National Aeronautics and Space Administration

NASA participates in the U.S. Telecommunications Training Institute for developing countries and conducts an international forum for regular exchanges between communications experts in developed and developing countries.

U.S. Postal Service

The Postal Service is a member of the Universal Postal Union. (See glossary entry.)

U.S. National Commission on UNESCO

(See glossary entry.)

Senate Committee on Commerce, Science and Transportation

1. Subcommittee on Communications--Deals with international communications aspects of regulatory and consumer affairs, and research and development policies.

Senate Committee on Foreign Relations

Various subcommittees, organized by world geographic areas deal with such aspects of international communications as technological cooperation; U.S. business interests overseas; international broadcasting; information, educational and cultural exchange.

House Committee on Foreign Affairs

The broad international jurisdiction of this

committee includes both technical and non-technical aspects of international communications through the following subcommittees:

1. Subcommittee on International Economic Policy and Trade;

2. Subcommittee on Human Rights and International Organizations;

3. Subcommittee on International Operations;

4. Subcommittee on International Security and Scientific Affairs.

House Committee on Energy and Commerce

1. Subcommittee on Telecommunications, Consumer Protection and Finance--Deals with telecommunications deregulation and competition in the U.S. and abroad; the productivity, technological standing and foreign trade potential of the U.S. information and communications industries.

House Committee on Government Operations

1. Subcommittee on Government Information and Individual Rights--Concerned with the organization and resources of the U.S. government in the fields of planning, policymaking and preparation for international conferences dealing with international communications.

House Committee on Science and Technology

This committee deals with international technical standards in communications; technology transfer and cooperation.

Index

Words and Phrases

Access to Information   4
Access to Media   5
Access to Sources   6
Advertising   7
Alternative Media   9
Censorship   10
Code of Ethics   12
Collaboration of Various Groups and Professional
   Communicators   13
Commercialization of Communications   14
Communications   15
Communications Infrastructures   15
Correct and Factual Information   16
Democratizing the Press   16
Developmental Journalism   17
Free and Balanced Flow of Information   18
Free Flow of Ideas by Word and Image   24
Free Flow of Information   24
Freedom of Information   21
Freedom of the Press   22
Harnessing the Power of Communication   25
Information   26
Information Gap   27
Information Infrastructure   28
International Information Law   30
Journalistic Pluralism   31
Licensing of Journalists   32
National Communications Policies   32

National News Agencies 33
Nationalization of Communications Technology 34
New World Information Order 37
News 34
News Monopoly 35
Normative Action 39
NWIO 39
Objectivity of the Press 39
Parachute Journalism 41
Pluralism 42
Process News 42
Progressive Incorporation of Communications
 Technology 43
Propaganda 44
Protection of Journalists 44
Protectionism in International Communications 45
Responsibility of the Press 46
Right to Communicate 47
Role of the Media 48
Sovereignty and International Communications 50
Taxation of Information Flow 50
Technology Transfer 50
Training of Journalists 50
Transnational Corporations 52

Organizations

AFP   54
Agence France-Presse   54
Agency for International Development   54
AID   54
American Newspapers Publishers Asociation   54
American Society of Newspaper Editors   55
ANPA   55
AP   55
Arab Revolutionary News Agency   55
ARNA   55
ASNE   56
Associated Press   56
Center for Strategic and International Studies   56
Communications Satellite Corporation   56
COMSAT   57
CSIS   57
ECOSOC   57
FCC   57
Federal Communications Commission   57
Freedom House   57
IAPA   58
IBI   58
IFRB   58
INEX   58
INTELSAT   58
Inter Press Service   62
Inter American Press Association   58
Intergovernmental Bureau of Informatics   58
International Commission for the Study of
    Communications Problems   59
International Press Institute   60
International Frequency Registration Board   59
International Organization of Journalists   59
International Program for the Development of
    Communication   60
International Telecommunications Satellite
    Organization   61
International Telecommunications Union   61
IOJ   62
IPDC   62

IPI 62
IPS 62
ITU 62
MacBride Commision 62
NANAP 62
National Telecommunication and Information Administration 63
News Agency Cooperatives 62
Nonaligned Press Agencies Pool 65
NTIA 64
OECD 64
Organization for Economic Co-operation and Development 64
RARC 64
Regional Administrative Radio Conference 64
Reuters 65
TASS 66
UN 66
UNCITRAL 66
UNCTAD 66
UNCTC 66
UNDP 66
UNESCO 67
United Nations 67
United Nations Commission on International Trade Law 67
United Nations Commission on Transnational Corporations 67
United Nations Conference on Trade and Development 68
United Nations Development Program 68
United Nations Economic and Social Council 69
United Nations Educational, Scientific, and Cultural Organization 69
United Press International 70
United States Department of State 70
United States Information Agency 71
United States National Commission for UNESCO 71
United States Trade Representative 71
Universal Postal Union 72
UPI 72
UPU 72

USIA 72
USTR 72
WARC 72
WPFC 73
World Administrative Radio Conference 72
World Press Freedom Committee 72

REF P96 .I5 B76

For Reference

Not to be taken from this room